SAGITTARIUS

With love to Bill, Jean, Rob and Shani

This is the third year that I've written these books and it's about time I thanked all the people who help me to put them together. I have worked with some of them since the beginning of the books, and others have only recently started lending me their help, but I am immensely grateful to them all. So thank you, Nova Jayne Heath, Nicola Chalton, Nick Robinson and everyone else at Robinson Publishing for being such a great team to work with. Thanks to Chelsey Fox for all her agenting skills. And a huge thank you to Annie Lionnet and Jamie Macphail for their tireless work.

SAGITTARIUS
2000

Jane Struthers

PARRAGON

First published in 1999 by Parragon

Parragon
Queen Street House
4 Queen Street
Bath BA1 1HE
UK

Produced by Magpie Books, an imprint of
Robinson Publishing Ltd, London

Illustrations courtesy of Slatter-Anderson, London

ISBN 0 75252 898 X

A copy of the British Library Cataloguing-in-Publication Data
is available from the British Library

Printed and bound in the EC

CONTENTS

Dates for 2000

Sagittarius 22 November – 20 December

Capricorn 21 December – 19 January

Aquarius 20 January – 18 February

Pisces 19 February – 19 March

Aries 20 March – 18 April

Taurus 19 April – 19 May

Gemini 20 May – 20 June

Cancer 21 June – 21 July

Leo 22 July – 21 August

Virgo 22 August – 21 September

Libra 22 September – 22 October

Scorpio 23 October – 21 November

YOUR SAGITTARIUS SUN SIGN

This chapter is all about your Sun sign. I'm going to describe your general personality, as well as the way you react in relationships, how you handle money, what your health is like and which careers suit you. But before I do all that, I want to explain what a Sun sign is. It's the sign that the Sun occupied at the time of your birth. Every year, the Sun moves through the sky, spending an average of 30 days in each of the signs. You're a Sagittarian, which means that you were born when the Sun was moving through the sign of Sagittarius. It's the same as saying that Sagittarius is your star sign, but astrologers prefer to use the term 'Sun sign' because it's more accurate.

Character

You are blessed with one of the most valuable characteristics of all – optimism. Your positive attitude to life is one of your greatest strengths and it has helped you to weather many storms. No matter how tough things are, you retain a positive attitude, your sense of humour and a strong belief that everything will turn out for the best. No wonder you're said to be the luckiest sign in the zodiac!

It's your ruler, Jupiter, that gives you such a life-enhancing attitude. Jupiter is the planet of good fortune and challenges. Sagittarius is the third of the Fire signs, which makes you expansive, enthusiastic and always keen to take the initiative and make things happen. And you certainly do that!

Life is always lively when you're around. You enjoy discussing ideas with friends and loved ones, especially if they involve a favourite topic or have philosophical, spiritual or political overtones. You're very intellectual and enjoy stretching your mind, so you probably have a home full of books and an extremely broad range of knowledge. You have a tremendous respect for knowledge and you spend your life learning more about people and the world around you.

Relationships

You take a great delight in getting to know people – you enjoy discovering what makes them tick and like sharing experiences. No wonder you have a lot of friends. People appreciate your open and straightforward manner because they know where they stand with you. After all, you're not the most tactful sign in the zodiac so it's awkward for you to be anything other than honest. You're usually found out because you let the cat out of the bag sooner or later.

The one thing you can't abide is feeling tied down or hemmed in by a partner. You need to be able to live your own life and not feel that someone is peering over your shoulder the whole time or trying to curb your freedom. If they do any of these things, you won't tolerate it for long and may even end the relationship if that's the only way to maintain a sense of independence. Although sex means a lot to you because it allows you to express your emotions, the most important requirement when looking for a partner is someone who will be a friend as well as a lover. You need a partner who'll still be your best friend long after the passion between you has simmered down, and whose intellect matches your own high standard. Anything less simply won't do.

Money

Money is very important to you. That's because you love spending it, so you need to earn it. Unfortunately, you're not very good at taking care of your cash, so you may have a rather slapdash approach to finance. Tedious details such as the state of your bank balance or the ebb and flow of direct debits through your account are about as exciting as last week's news. You tell yourself that you've got more important things to think about, although you sometimes face a monetary crisis when you're forced to take action.

As far as you're concerned, the most exciting thing about money is what it can buy you. Books, for a start, as well as plane tickets so you can indulge your love of travel with lots of adventurous holidays. You're not so keen on buying expensive possessions that act as status symbols – you much prefer wearing casual clothes to anything very formal so you're not particularly impressed by designer labels. However, you would enjoy owning a fast car that's sleek and very distinctive. Your ideal is to have enough money to be free to do whatever you want with your life.

Health

You're one of the most active signs of all, and if you're a typical Sagittarian you enjoy keeping on the move. You may get plenty of exercise simply because you find it hard to sit still and you're always dashing hither and thither.

The more sedentary your life, the more restless you feel, although you're probably not keen on taking exercise just for the sake of it. You need to find an activity that engages your brain as well as your body. You enjoy walking, although your busy schedule may mean you spend more time in the car or behind a desk than pounding the pavements. Try to reverse this trend whenever possible. You really benefit from being in the wide open spaces and breathing plenty of fresh air. Among the activities that could appeal are horse-riding (your sign is noted for its love of horses), squash, motor-racing and any other sport that requires steel nerves and a dare-devil attitude. As a result, you can often strain muscles, especially if the pursuits you choose are dangerous or strenuous.

For a Sagittarian, the vulnerable areas of the body are the hips and liver. When you put on weight, it's most likely to centre around your hips and can be increasingly hard to shift as the years go by. You thoroughly enjoy eating and drinking, which means that your liver can suffer, especially if you eat a lot of rich food.

Career

Because you're one of the most intellectual signs in the zodiac, ideally you should choose a career that gives your mind plenty of scope and, preferably, presents a challenge. You hate the thought of a job that's dreary, monotonous or so mindless that you just switch off while you're doing it. Anything that smacks of routine will soon make you feel fed up. Instead, you need an occupation that allows you continually to learn more about the world and to add to your store of knowledge. Sagittarians are born teachers, so if you can impart some of your experience to other people even in very informal ways you'll feel satisfied and content. You also need a job that keeps you on the move: being stuck behind a desk or permanently at a shop counter will soon start to frustrate you. If you can also meet plenty of interesting people, you'll be really happy.

Ideal Sagittarian professions include education, publishing, writing, broadcasting, religion, philosophy and travel. Although you're not particularly ambitious, you do like to have a sense of achievement and to know that you're getting a lot out of your work and also that you're putting a lot into it.

MERCURY AND YOUR COMMUNICATIONS

Where would we be without Mercury? This tiny planet rules everything connected with our communications, from the way we speak to the way we get about. The position of Mercury in your birth chart describes how fast or how slow you absorb information, the sorts of things you talk about, the way you communicate with other people and how much nervous energy you have.

Mercury is an important part of everyone's birth chart, but it has extra meaning for Geminis and Virgos because both these signs are ruled by Mercury.

Mercury is the closest planet to the Sun in the solar system, and its orbit lies between the Earth and the Sun. In fact, it is never more than 28 degrees away from the Sun. Mercury is one of the smallest known planets in the solar system, but it makes up in speed what it lacks in size. It whizzes around the Sun at about 108,000 miles an hour, to avoid being sucked into the Sun's fiery mass.

If you've always wondered how astrology works, here's a brief explanation. Your horoscope (a map of the planets' positions at the time of your birth) is divided up into twelve sections, known as 'houses'. Each one represents a different area of your life, and together they cover every aspect of our experiences on Earth. As Mercury moves around the heavens each year it progresses through each house in turn, affecting a particular part of your life, such as your health or career. If you plot its progress through your own chart, you'll be able to make the most of Mercury's influence in 2000. That way, you'll know when it's best to make contact with others and when it's wisest to keep your thoughts to yourself.

Mercury takes just over one year to complete its orbit of the Earth, but during this time it doesn't always travel forwards, it also appears to go backwards. When this happens, it means that, from our vantage point on Earth, Mercury has slowed down to such an extent that it seems to be backtracking through the skies. We call this retrograde motion. When Mercury is travelling forwards, we call it direct motion.

All the planets, with the exception of the Sun and Moon, go retrograde at some point during their orbit of the Earth. A retrograde Mercury is very important because it means that during this time our communications can hit delays and snags. Messages may go missing, letters could get lost in the post, appliances and gadgets can go on the blink. You may also find it hard to make yourself understood. In 2000, there are several periods when Mercury goes retrograde. These are between 21 February and 14 March, 23 June and 17 July, and between 18 October and 8 November. These are all times to keep a close eye on your communications. You may also feel happiest if you can avoid signing important agreements or contracts during these times.

To plot the progress of Mercury, fill in the blank diagram on page 8, writing '1' in the section next to your Sun sign, then numbering consecutively in an anti-clockwise direction around the signs until you have completed them all. It will now be easy to chart Mercury's movements. When it is in the same sign as your Sun, Mercury is in your first house, when he moves into the next sign (assuming he's not going retrograde) he occupies your second house, and so on, until he reaches your twelfth house, at which point he will move back into your first house again.

Diagram 1

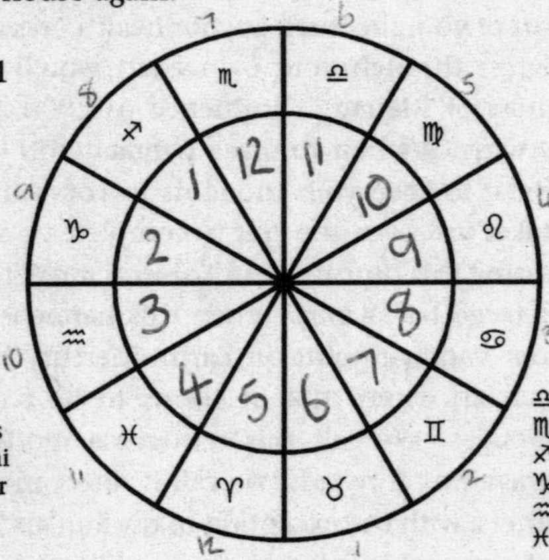

♈ – Aries
♉ – Taurus
♊ – Gemini
♋ – Cancer
♌ – Leo
♍ – Virgo

♎ – Libra
♏ – Scorpio
♐ – Sagittarius
♑ – Capricorn
♒ – Aquarius
♓ – Pisces

Here are the houses of the horoscope, numbered from one to twelve, for someone born with the Sun in Aquarius.

Diagram 2

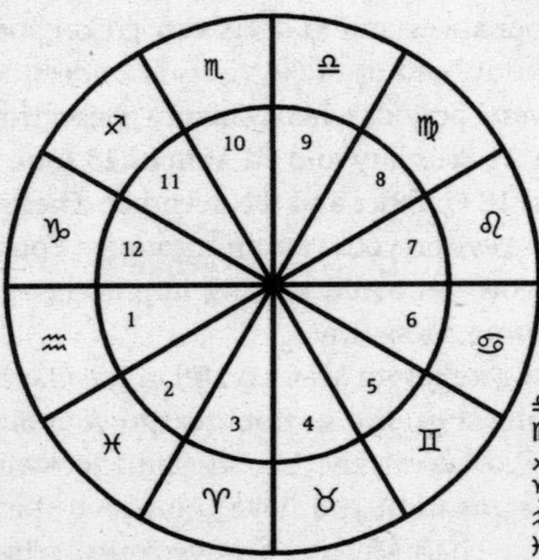

♈ – Aries
♉ – Taurus
♊ – Gemini
♋ – Cancer
♌ – Leo
♍ – Virgo

♎ – Libra
♏ – Scorpio
♐ – Sagittarius
♑ – Capricorn
♒ – Aquarius
♓ – Pisces

MERCURY'S ENTRY INTO THE SIGNS IN 2000
(All times are given in GMT, using the 24-hour clock)

January
Mercury is in Capricorn when 2000 begins

18	22:21	Aquarius

February

5	08:10	Pisces
21	12:47	Retrograde in Pisces

March

14	20:40	Direct in Pisces

April

13	00:18	Aries
30	03:54	Taurus

May

14	07:11	Gemini
30	04:28	Cancer

June

23	08:33	Retrograde in Cancer

July

17	13:21	Direct in Cancer

August

7	05:43	Leo
22	10:12	Virgo

September

7	21:23	Libra
28	13:29	Scorpio

October

18	13:42	Retrograde in Scorpio

November		
7	07:29	Retrograde into Libra
8	02:29	Direct in Libra
8	21:43	Scorpio

December		
3	20:27	Sagittarius
23	02:04	Capricorn

As 2000 begins, Mercury is moving through the final degrees of Capricorn, so it is in whichever house corresponds with the sign of Capricorn in your diagram. For instance, if you're an Aquarian, Mercury will move into your own sign at 22:21 GMT on 18 January and will occupy your first house. You can then read the explanation below telling you what to expect at this time. Mercury next moves signs at 08:10 GMT on 5 February, when he moves into Pisces. So if you're an Aquarian, Mercury will now be in your second house.

Mercury in the First House

This is a very busy time for you and you're completely wrapped up in your own ideas and concerns. Even if you aren't usually very chatty, you certainly are at the moment. However, you will much prefer talking about yourself to listening to other people! You've got lots of nervous energy at the moment and you'll enjoy getting out and about as much as possible. Look for ways of burning off excess energy, such as going for brisk walks or doing things that require initiative. This is a great opportunity to think about ways of pushing forward with ideas and getting new projects off the ground.

Mercury in the Second House

This is a great time to think about things that mean a lot to you. These might be beliefs, philosophies or anything else that gives meaning to your life. It's also a good time to consider the people that make your world go round. Do you devote enough time to them? You should also spare a thought for your finances, because this is a perfect opportunity to scrutinize them and make sure everything is in order. You could get in touch with someone who can give you some financial advice, or you might do some research into how to put your money to good use.

Mercury in the Third House

Chatty? You bet! This is probably when you're at your most talkative, and you'll enjoy nattering away about whatever pops into your head. You'll love talking to whoever happens to be around, but you'll get on especially well with neighbours, people you see in the course of your daily routine and close relatives. You'll soon start to feel restless if you have to spend too long in one place, so grab every opportunity to vary your schedule. You'll love taking off on day trips, going away for weekend breaks or simply abandoning your usual routine and doing something completely different. Communications will go well and you'll love playing with gadgets and appliances.

Mercury in the Fourth House

Your thoughts are never far away from your home and family life at the moment. You may be thinking about ways of improving your living standards and you could talk to people who can give you some advice. You're also wrapped up in thoughts of the past, and you may even be assailed by memories of far-off events or things you haven't thought about in ages. Pay attention to your dreams because they could give you some invaluable insights into the way you're feeling. Watch out for a slight tendency to be defensive or to imagine that people are trying to get at you. It's a lovely time for getting in touch with your nearest and dearest who live a long way away.

Mercury in the Fifth House

You'll really enjoy putting your mind to good use at the moment, especially if you do things that are based on fun. For instance, you might get engrossed in competitions, jigsaw puzzles, crosswords and quizzes, especially if there's the chance of winning a prize! Children and pets will be terrific company and you'll love romping with them. However, you may find that they're a lot more playful than usual. You may even be on the receiving end of some practical jokes. It's a super time to go on holiday, particularly if you're visiting somewhere you've never been before. Your social life promises to keep you busy and you'll find it easy to talk to loved ones about things that matter to you.

Mercury in the Sixth House

This is the ideal time of year to think about your health and well-being. Are you looking after yourself properly? If you've been battling with some strange symptoms, this is the perfect opportunity to get them investigated so you can put your mind at rest. You'll enjoy reading about medical matters, such as immersing yourself in a book that tells you how to keep fit or extolling the virtues of a specific eating plan. Your work might also keep you busy. Colleagues and customers will be chatty, and you could spend a lot of time dealing with paperwork or tapping away on the computer. It's a great time to look for a new job, especially if that means scanning the newspaper adverts, joining an employment agency or writing lots of application letters.

Mercury in the Seventh House

Communications play an important role in all your relationships at the moment. This is your chance to put across your point of view and to keep other people posted about what you think. You may enjoy having lots of chats with partners or you might have something important to discuss. Either way, the key to success is to keep talking! You're prepared to reach a compromise, so it's a marvellous time to get involved in negotiations and discussions. You'll also find that two heads are better than one right now, so it's the ideal time to do some teamwork. You'll enjoy bouncing your ideas off other people and listening to what they have to say.

Mercury in the Eighth House

It's time to turn your attention to your shared resources and official money matters. So if you share a bank account with your partner, you should check that everything is running smoothly. You might even decide to open a new account that suits you better or that pays a higher rate of interest. Speaking of accounts, this is an excellent time to fill in your tax return or complete your accounts for the year because you're in the right frame of mind for such things. This is also a good time to think about your close relationships. Do they bring you the emotional satisfaction that you need or is something missing? If you think there's room for improvement, talk to your partner about how to make things better between you.

Mercury in the Ninth House

The more you can expand your mental and physical horizons now, the happier you'll be. It's a time of year when you're filled with intellectual curiosity about the world and you long to cram your head with all sorts of facts and figures. You might decide to do some studying, whether you do it on a very informal basis or enrol for an evening class or college course. You'll certainly enjoy browsing around bookshops and library shelves, looking for books on your favourite subjects. Travel will appeal to you too, especially if you can visit somewhere exotic or a place that you've never been to before. You might become interested in a different religion from your own or you could be engrossed in something connected with philosophy, history or spirituality.

Mercury in the Tenth House

Spend some time thinking about your career prospects. Are you happy with the way things are going or does your professional life need a rethink? This is a great opportunity to talk to people who can give you some good advice. It's also an excellent time to share your ideas with your boss or a superior, especially if you're hoping to impress them. You could hear about a promotion or some improved job prospects, or you might decide to apply for a completely new job. It's also a marvellous opportunity to increase your qualifications, perhaps by training for something new or brushing up on an existing skill. You'll find it easier than usual to talk to older friends and relatives, especially if they can sometimes be a little tricky or hard to please.

Mercury in the Eleventh House

This is a great time to enjoy the company of friends and acquaintances. You'll love talking to them, especially if you can chat about subjects that make you think or that have humanitarian overtones. All sorts of intellectual activities will appeal to you at the moment. If your social circle is getting smaller and smaller, grab this chance to widen your horizons by meeting people who are on the same wavelength as you. For instance, you might decide to join a new club or society that caters for one of your interests. It's also a good opportunity to think about your hopes and wishes for the future. Are they going according to plan, or should you revise your strategy or even start again from scratch?

Mercury in the Twelfth House

You're entering a very reflective and reclusive period when you want to retreat from the madding crowd and have some time to yourself. You might enjoy taking the phone off the hook and curling up with a good book, or you could spend time studying subjects by yourself. There will be times when you feel quite tongue-tied, and you'll find it difficult to say exactly what you mean. You may even want to maintain a discreet silence on certain subjects, but make sure that other people don't take advantage of this by putting words into your mouth. You could be the recipient of someone's confidences, in which case you'll be a sympathetic listener. If you want to tell someone your secrets, choose your confidante wisely.

LOVE AND THE STARS

Love makes the world go round. When we know we're loved, we walk on air. We feel confident, happy and joyous. Without love, we feel miserable, lonely and as if life isn't worth living. If you're still looking for your perfect partner, this is the ideal guide for you. It will tell you which Sun signs you get on best with and which ones aren't such easy-going mates. By the way, there is hope for every astrological combination, and none are out and out disasters. It's simply that you'll find it easier to get on well with some signs than with others.

At the end of this section you'll see two compatibility charts – one showing how you get on in the love and sex stakes, and the other one telling you which signs make the best friends. These charts will instantly remind you which signs get on best and which struggle to keep the peace. Each combination has been given marks out of ten, with ten points being a fabulous pairing and one point being pretty grim. Find the woman's Sun sign along the top line of the chart, then look down the left-hand column for the man's sign. The square where these two lines meet will give you the result of this astrological combination. For instance, when assessing the love and sex compatibility of a Leo woman and a Cancerian man, they score six out of ten.

Sagittarius

When a Sagittarian pairs up with a fellow Fire sign, there's plenty of warmth and the odd firework. A Sagittarian is thrilled by the adventurous spirit of an Arien, and they love exploring the world together. There are plenty of tall tales when a Sagittarian gets together with a Leo – they'll try to outdo each other, dropping names and recounting their greatest triumphs. If the Leo is slightly pompous, the Sagittarian is able to take them down a peg or two, but they must beware of hurting the Leo's feelings. As for two Sagittarians, they'll spur each other on and encourage one another to gain as much experience of life as possible. You probably won't be able to move in their house for books.

With their endless curiosity about the world, Sagittarians understand the intellectual Air signs very well. A Sagittarian enjoys the chatty company of a Gemini and, because they're opposite numbers in the zodiac, the Sagittarian is able to encourage the Gemini to see things through and explore them in more detail than usual. A refined and diplomatic Libran will try to teach the blunt Sagittarian not to say the first thing that pops into their head. However, the Sagittarian may eventually find the Libran's sense of balance rather trying – why can't they get more worked up about things? There's plenty of straight talking when a Sagittarian teams up with an Aquarian – they both have a high regard for honesty. The independent Sagittarian respects the Aquarian's need for freedom, but may feel rather stung by their periods of emotional coolness.

A Sagittarian will struggle to understand the Earth signs. They respect the Taurean's ability to work hard but they're driven to distraction by their reluctance to make changes and break out of any ruts they've fallen into. A Sagittarian enjoys talking to a brainy Virgo, but their expansive and spontaneous nature could eventually be restricted by the Virgo's need to think things through before taking action. When a Sagittarian gets together with a Capricorn, it's a case of optimism versus pessimism. While the Sagittarian's glass is half-full, the Capricorn's is always half-empty, and this causes many rows and possibly some ill feeling.

There could be lots of misunderstandings when a Sagittarian gets involved with one of the Water signs. A Sagittarian needs a bigger social circle than their family, whereas a Cancerian is quite happy surrounded by kith and kin. The Sagittarian need for independence won't go down well, either. It's like oil and water when a Sagittarian pairs up with a Scorpio. The Sagittarian is the roamer of the zodiac, whereas the Scorpio wants them where they can see them, in case they're up to no good. All will be well if the Sagittarian gets together with a strong-minded Piscean. In fact, they'll really enjoy one another's company. A Piscean who's lost in a world of their own, however, will soon leave them cold.

Capricorn

Despite their outward poise, a Capricorn is very easily hurt so they need to know their feelings won't be trampled on. There's least danger of that when they get together with a fellow Earth sign. A Capricorn adores a Taurean's deep sense of responsibility and they'll both work hard to create their ideal home. A Capricorn appreciates the methodical approach of a Virgo, but could feel deeply hurt by the Virgo's sharp tongue and caustic remarks. If two Capricorns team up, one of them must be demonstrative and openly affectionate otherwise the relationship could be rather sterile and serious.

Capricorns also feel safe with members of the Water signs. When a Capricorn gets together with a Cancerian, they do their utmost to make their home a haven. They'll get great satisfaction from channelling their energies into bringing up a family. A Capricorn may be rather bemused by the depth and intensity of a Scorpio's emotions – Capricorns are too reserved to indulge in such drama themselves and it can make them feel uncomfortable. A no-nonsense Capricorn could be perplexed by an extremely vulnerable Piscean and won't know how to handle them. Should they give them a hanky or tell them to pull themselves together?

The Air signs can also make a Capricorn feel somewhat unsettled. They're fascinated by a Gemini's breadth of knowledge and endless chat, but they also find them superficial and rather flighty. In fact, the Capricorn probably doesn't trust the Gemini. A Capricorn feels far happier in the company of a Libran. Here's someone who seems much steadier emotionally and who can help the Capricorn to unwind after a hard day's work. It can be great or ghastly when a Capricorn sets their sights on an Aquarian. They understand each other provided the Aquarian isn't too unconventional, but the Capricorn feels uncomfortable and embarrassed by any displays of eccentricity, deliberate or not.

The Fire signs help to warm up the Capricorn, who can be rather remote and distant at times. A Capricorn admires the Arien's drive and initiative, but endlessly tells them to look before they leap and could become irritated when they don't take this sage advice. When a Capricorn gets together with a Leo, they won't need to worry about appearances – the Capricorn will feel justly proud of the smart Leo. However, they could wince when the bills come in and they discover how much those clothes cost. A Capricorn thinks a Sagittarian must have come from another planet – how can they be so relaxed and laid-back all the time? They have great respect for the Sagittarian's wisdom and philosophy, but they quickly become fed up with having to fit in around the Sagittarian's hectic social life.

Aquarius

Put an Aquarian with a fellow Air sign and they're happy. They thoroughly enjoy being with a lively Gemini and love discussing everything under the sun with them. They may not have a very exciting sex life, but their mental closeness will more than make up for it. The gentle charms of a Libran calms down an Aquarian when their nerves become frayed, although they disapprove of the Libran's innate tact and diplomacy – why can't they just say what they think, instead of sitting on the fence? With two Aquarians you never know what to expect, other than that they'll be great friends. They'll certainly do a lot of talking, but could spend more time debating esoteric ideas and abstract concepts.

An Aquarian likes all the Fire signs, although they find Ariens hard to fathom and can become exhausted by an Arien's endless supply of energy and enthusiasm. There are no such problems when an Aquarian pairs up with a Leo because they complement each other in many ways. The Aquarian teaches objectivity to the Leo, who in return encourages the Aquarian to express their emotions more. An Aquarian thoroughly enjoys being with a Sagittarian because both of them hate being tied down. As a result, they respect one another's independence and will probably rarely see each other because of all their spare-time activities.

It's not quite so simple when an Aquarian joins forces with one of the Earth signs. An Aquarian will lock horns with a Taurean sooner or later, because neither of them is able to back down once a disagreement has started. The Aquarian will also feel very restricted by the Taurean's possessiveness. The Virgo's analytical approach to life intrigues the Aquarian but they'll sit up all night arguing the toss over everything, with each one convinced that they've got all the answers. When an Aquarian meets a Capricorn, they've got their work cut out for them if they're to find a happy medium between the erratic Aquarian and the conventional Capricorn.

An Aquarian feels out of their depth when they're with one of the Water signs. They simply don't understand what makes a Cancerian tick – why do they worry themselves sick over things that they can't change? The Aquarian finds it all most peculiar. They also find it difficult to understand a Scorpio who takes so many things so seriously. Although the Aquarian also has a list of topics that mean a lot to them, they're not the sort of things that hold the slightest interest for a Scorpio. It's more or less the same story with a Pisces, because their huge resources of emotion make the Aquarian feel uncomfortable and fill them with a strong desire to escape as fast as possible.

Pisces

Relationships mean a lot to a sensitive Piscean, but they're easily misunderstood by many of the more robust signs. There are no such worries with the other Water signs, however. A Piscean loves being with a tender Cancerian who knows how to help them relax and feel safe. They really enjoy playing house together but the emotional scenes will blow the roof off. The relationship between a Piscean and a Scorpio can be quite spicy and sexy, but the Piscean is turned off if the Scorpio becomes too intense and dramatic. Two Pisceans feel safe with one another, but they'll push all their problems under the carpet unless one of them is more objective.

A Piscean also gets on well with the Earth signs, although with a few reservations. A Piscean takes comfort from being looked after by a protective Taurean, but after a while they could feel stifled by the Taurean's possessive and matter-of-fact attitude. The relationship between a Piscean and a Virgo starts off well but the Piscean could soon feel crushed by the Virgo's criticism and will need more emotional reassurance than the Virgo is able to give. A Piscean feels safe with a Capricorn because they're so dependable but in the end this may begin to bug them. It's not that they want the Capricorn to two-time them, more that they'd like a little unpredictability every now and then.

A Piscean is fascinated by the Air signs but their apparent lack of emotion could cause problems. A Piscean and a Gemini are terrific friends but could encounter difficulties as lovers. The Piscean's strong emotional needs are too much for the Gemini to handle – they'll feel as if they're drowning. The Piscean is on much firmer ground with a Libran, who'll go out of their way to keep the Piscean happy. Neither sign is good at facing up to any nasty truths, however. An Aquarian is too much for a sensitive Piscean, who views the world through rose-coloured specs. An Aquarian, on the other hand, has uncomfortably clear vision.

The Fire signs can cheer up a Piscean enormously, but any prolonged displays of emotion will make the Fire signs feel weighed down. The Piscean is fascinated by an Arien's exploits but could feel reluctant to join in. They'll also be easily hurt by some of the Arien's off-the-cuff remarks. When a Piscean pairs up with a Leo they appreciate the way the Leo wants to take charge and look after them. After a while, however, this could grate on them and they'll want to be more independent. A Piscean enjoys discussing philosophy and spiritual ideas with a Sagittarian – they can sit up half the night talking things through. The Sagittarian brand of honesty could hurt the Piscean at times, but they know this isn't malicious and will quickly forgive such outbursts.

Aries

Because Ariens belong to the Fire element, they get on very well with their fellow Fire signs Leo and Sagittarius. All the same, an Arien getting together with a Leo will soon notice a distinct drop in their bank balance, because they'll enjoy going to all the swankiest restaurants and sitting in the best seats at the theatre. When an Arien pairs up with a Sagittarian, they'll compete over who drives the fastest car and has the most exciting holidays. When two Ariens get together the results can be combustible. Ideally, one Arien should be a lot quieter, otherwise they'll spend most of their time jostling for power. All these combinations are very sexy and physical.

Ariens also thrive in the company of the three Air signs – Gemini, Libra and Aquarius. Of the three, they get on best with Geminis, who share their rather childlike view of the world and also their sense of fun. An Arien and a Gemini enjoy hatching all sorts of ideas and schemes, even if they never get round to putting them into action. There's an exciting sense of friction between Aries and Libra, their opposite number in the zodiac. An Arien will be enchanted by the way their Libran caters to their every need, but may become impatient when the Libran also wants to look after other people. An Arien will be captivated by the originality of an Aquarian, although at times they'll be driven mad by the Aquarian's eccentric approach to life and the way they blow hot and cold in the bedroom.

Ariens don't do so well with the Earth signs – Taurus, Virgo and Capricorn. The very careful, slightly plodding nature of a typical Taurean can drive an Arien barmy at times, and although they'll respect – and benefit from – the Taurean's practical approach to life, it can still fill them with irritation. An Arien finds it difficult to fathom a Virgo, because their attitudes to life are diametrically opposed. An Arien likes to jump in with both feet, while a Virgo prefers to take things slowly and analyse every possibility before committing themselves. An Arien can get on quite well with a Capricorn, because they're linked by their sense of ambition and their earthy sexual needs.

An Arien is out of their depth with any of the Water signs – Cancer, Scorpio and Pisces. They quickly become irritated by the defensive Cancerian, although they'll love their cooking. An Arien will enjoy a very passionate affair with a Scorpio, but the Scorpio's need to know exactly what the Arien is up to when their back is turned will soon cause problems and rifts. Although an Arien may begin a relationship with a Pisces by wanting to look after them and protect them from the harsh realities of life, eventually the Piscean's extremely sensitive nature may bring out the Arien's bullying streak.

Taurus

Taureans are literally in their element when they're with Virgos or Capricorns who, like themselves, are Earth signs. Two Taureans will get along very happily together, although they could become so wedded to routine that they get stuck in a rut. They may also encourage one another to eat too much. A Taurean will enjoy being with a Virgo, because they respect the Virgo's methodical nature. They'll also like encouraging their Virgo to relax and take life easy. Money will form a link between a Taurean and a Capricorn, with plenty of serious discussions on how to make it and what to do with it once they've got it. There will also be a strong sexual rapport, and the Taurean will encourage the more sensual side of the Capricorn.

The relationship between a Taurean and members of the Water element is also very good. A Taurean and a Cancerian will revel in one another's company and will probably be so happy at home that they'll rarely stir from their armchairs. They both have a strong need for emotional security and will stick together through thick and thin. There's plenty of passion when a Taurean pairs up with a Scorpio, although the faithful Taurean could become fed up with the Scorpio's jealous nature. They simply won't understand what they're being accused of, and their loyal nature will be offended by the very thought that they could be a two-timer. A Taurean will be delighted by a delicate Piscean, and will want to take care of such a vulnerable and sensitive creature.

Things become rather more complicated when a Taurean pairs up with an Arien, Leo or Sagittarian, all of whom are Fire signs. They have very little in common – Taureans like to take things slowly while Fire signs want to make things happen *now*. It's particularly difficult between a Taurean and an Arien – the careful Taurean will feel harried and rushed by the impetuous Arien. It's a little better when a Taurean gets together with a Leo, because they share a deep appreciation of the good things in life, although the Taurean will be horrified by the Leo's ability to spend money. Making joint decisions could be difficult, however, because they'll both stand their ground and refuse to budge. A Taurean and a Sagittarian simply don't understand each other – they're on such different wavelengths. Any Taurean displays of possessiveness will make the independent Sagittarian want to run a mile.

Taureans are equally mystified by the Air signs – Gemini, Libra and Aquarius. What they see as the flightiness of Gemini drives them barmy – why can't the Gemini settle down and do one thing at a time? The Taurean will probably feel quite exhausted by the Gemini's many interests and bubbly character. Taurus and Libra are a surprisingly good pairing, because they share a need for beauty, luxury and love. This could end up costing the penny-wise Taurean quite a packet, but they'll have a deliciously romantic time along the way. Taurus and Aquarius are chalk and cheese, and neither one is prepared to meet the other one halfway. The Taurean need to keep tabs on their loved one's every movement will irritate the freedom-loving Aquarian, and there will be plenty of rows as a result.

Gemini

One of the Air signs, Geminis get on very well with their fellow members of this element – Librans and Aquarians. Two Geminis are the astrological equivalent of double trouble – they chat nineteen to the dozen and revel in the company of someone who understands them so well. A Gemini delights in being with a Libran, because they enjoy the intellectual company and will benefit from the Libran's (usually) relaxed approach to life. They'll also learn to deal with their emotions more if a sympathetic Libran can guide them. Gemini and Aquarius is a very exciting pairing – the Gemini is encouraged to think deeply and knows that the Aquarian won't put up with any woolly ideas or fudged arguments.

Geminis also get on well with the three Fire signs – Aries, Leo and Sagittarius. A Gemini loves being with a racy, adventurous Arien, and together they enjoy keeping abreast of all the latest gossip and cultural developments. However, after the first flush of enthusiasm has worn off, the Gemini may find the Arien's strong need for sex rather hard to take. The Gemini gets on very well with a Leo. They delight in the Leo's affectionate nature and are amused by their need to have the best that money can buy – and they'll gladly share in the spoils. Gemini and Sagittarius are an excellent combination, because they sit opposite each other in the zodiac and so complement one another's character. The Gemini will be fascinated by the erudite and knowledgeable Sagittarian.

Gemini doesn't do so well with the Earth signs of Taurus and Capricorn, although they get on better with Virgo. The Gemini finds it difficult to understand a Taurean, because they see the world from such different viewpoints. The Gemini takes a more light-hearted approach and lives life at such a speed that they find it difficult to slow down to the more measured pace of a Taurean. The wonderfully dry Capricorn sense of humour is a source of constant delight to a Gemini. However, they're less taken with the Capricorn's streak of pessimism and their love of tradition. Of the three Earth signs, Gemini and Virgo are the most compatible. The Gemini shares the Virgo's brainpower and they have long, fascinating conversations.

When a Gemini gets together with the Water signs, the result can be enjoyable or puzzling. Gemini and Cancer have little in common, because the Gemini wants to spread their emotional and intellectual wings, whereas a Cancerian likes to stay close to home and has little interest in abstract ideas. Gemini finds Scorpio perplexing because they operate on such different levels. A Gemini tends to skim along the surface of things, so often deals with life on a superficial level, whereas a Scorpio likes to dig deep and has to have an emotional investment in everything they do. A Gemini appreciates the subtlety and sensitivity of a Piscean, but they're likely to make off-the-cuff comments that unwittingly hurt the Piscean.

Cancer

Cancerians revel in the company of their fellow Water signs of Scorpio and Pisces. When two Cancerians get together they could spend most of their time at home or eating – preferably both. They feel safe in the knowledge that they both have a strong need for love, but their innate Cancerian tenacity may mean they cling on to the relationship even if it's long past its best. A Cancerian is enchanted with a Scorpio, because at last they feel free to really let rip emotionally. However, the intuitive Cancerian should beware of soaking up the Scorpio's darker moods like a psychic sponge. A Cancerian will take one look at a delicate Piscean and want to invite them home for a good hot meal. All the Cancerian's protective instincts are aroused by a gentle Piscean, but their anger will also be aroused if it turns out the Piscean has been leading a double life behind their back.

Cancerians also find a great deal of comfort in the company of the Earth signs – Taurus, Virgo and Capricorn. Cancer and Taurus were made for each other – they both adore home comforts and they trust one another implicitly. The Cancerian loves making a cosy nest for their hard-working Taurean. A Cancerian finds a Virgo a more difficult proposition, especially emotionally. Whereas Cancer is all warm hugs and holding hands by the fire, Virgo prefers to read a book and reserve any displays of affection for the bedroom. Cancer and Capricorn are opposite numbers in the zodiac, so share a tremendous rapport. They also share the same values of home, tradition and family, and if anyone can help a Capricorn to relax and take life easy, it's a Cancerian.

Life becomes more difficult when it comes to a Cancerian's relationship with any of the Air signs. They simply don't understand one another. A Cancerian can't make a Gemini out. They feel confused by what they think of as the Gemini's flightiness and inability to stay in one place for long. They can also be easily hurt by the Gemini's difficulty in expressing their emotions. A Cancerian gets on much better with a Libran. They're both ambitious in their own ways and so have a great deal in common. The Cancerian enjoys the Libran's romantic nature, but the Cancerian tendency to cling doesn't go down well. A Cancerian regards a typical Aquarian as a being from another planet. They're hurt by the Aquarian's strong need for independence and dislike of having to account for their every action, and are dismayed and confused by the Aquarian's hot-and-cold attitude to sex.

The Fire signs of Aries, Leo and Sagittarius are also a potential source of bewilderment to the gentle Cancerian. They understand the drive and ambition of an Arien, but will be stung by their blunt speech and worried about their daredevil tendencies. What if they hurt themselves? A Cancerian gets on well with a Leo because they share a strong love of family and are both openly affectionate and loving. The Cancerian enjoys creating a home that the Leo can feel proud of. So far, so good, but the story isn't so simple when a Cancerian pairs up with a Sagittarian. They're too different to understand one another – the Cancerian wants to stay at home with the family while the Sagittarian has an instinctive need to roam the world. As a result, the Cancerian will be disappointed, and then hurt, when the Sagittarian's busy schedule takes them away from home too often.

Leo

Leos adore the company of their fellow Fire signs, Ariens and Sagittarius. They understand one another and enjoy each other's spontaneous warmth and affection. A Leo is amused by the exuberance and impulsiveness of an Arien, and they enjoy being persuaded to let their hair down a bit and not worry too much about appearances. A Leo enjoys the dash and vitality of a Sagittarian, although they may feel irritated if they can never get hold of them on the phone or the Sagittarian is always off doing other things. Two Leos together either love or loathe one another. One of them should be prepared to take a back seat otherwise they'll both be vying for the limelight all the time.

The three Air signs of Gemini, Libra and Aquarius all get on well with Leos. When a Leo pairs up with a Gemini, you can expect lots of laughter and plenty of fascinating conversations. The demonstrative Leo is able to help the Gemini be more openly affectionate and loving. Leo and Libra is a great combination, and the Leo is enchanted by the Libran's fair-minded attitude. Both signs love luxury and all the good things in life but their bank managers may not be so pleased by the amount of the money they manage to spend. Leo and Aquarius sit opposite one another across the horoscope, so they already have a great deal in common. They're fascinated by one another but they're both very stubborn, so any disputes between them usually end in stalemate because neither is prepared to concede any ground.

Leos don't really understand the Earth signs. Although Leos admire their practical approach to life, they find it rather restricting. A Leo enjoys the sensuous and hedonistic side of a Taurean's character but may become frustrated by their fear of change. Leo and Virgo have very little in common, especially when it comes to food – the Leo wants to tuck in at all the best restaurants while the Virgo is worried about the state of the kitchens, the number of calories and the size of the bill. A Leo respects the Capricorn's desire to support their family and approves of their need to be seen in the best possible light, but they feel hurt by the Capricorn's difficulty in showing their feelings.

When a Leo gets together with one of the Water signs – Cancer, Scorpio or Pisces – they'll enjoy the sexual side of the relationship but could eventually feel stifled by all that Watery emotion. A Leo and a Cancerian adore making a home together and both dote on their children. The Leo also likes comforting their vulnerable Cancerian – provided this doesn't happen too often. A Leo and a Scorpio will be powerfully attracted to one another, but power could also pull them apart – who's going to wear the trousers? They'll also lock horns during rows and both of them will refuse to back down. A Leo delights in a sophisticated Piscean, but may become irritated by their indecision and jangly nerves.

Virgo

As you might imagine, Virgos are happy with their fellow Earth signs of Taurus and Capricorn because they share the same practical attitude. A Virgo enjoys the steady, reassuring company of a Taurean, and they might even learn to relax a little instead of worrying themselves into the ground over the slightest problem. When two Virgos get together it can be too much of a good thing. Although at first they'll love talking to someone who shares so many of their preoccupations and ideas, they can soon drive one another round the bend. When a Virgo first meets a Capricorn they're delighted to know someone who's obviously got their head screwed on. It's only later on that they wish the Capricorn could lighten up every now and then.

Virgos get on well with Cancerians, Scorpios and Pisceans, the three Water signs. A Virgo enjoys being looked after by a considerate Cancerian, although they'll worry about their waistline and may get irritated by the Cancerian's super-sensitive feelings. You can expect plenty of long, analytical conversations when a Virgo gets together with a Scorpio. They both love getting to the bottom of subjects and will endlessly talk things through. They'll also get on extremely well in the bedroom. Pisces is Virgo's opposite sign, but although some opposites thrive in each other's company, that isn't always the case with this combination. The Virgo could soon grow impatient with the dreamy Piscean and will long to tell them a few home truths.

Although the other Earth signs don't usually get on well with Air signs, it's different for Virgos. They understand the intellectual energies of Geminis, Librans and Aquarians. A Virgo thrives in a Gemini's company, and they spend hours chatting over the phone if they can't get together in person. It's difficult for them to discuss their emotions, however, and they may never tell each other how they really feel. A Virgo admires a sophisticated, charming Libran, and marvels at their diplomacy. How do they do it? Expect a few sparks to fly when a Virgo pairs up with an Aquarian, because both of them have very strong opinions and aren't afraid to air them. The result is a lot of hot air and some vigorous arguments.

The three Fire signs – Aries, Leo and Sagittarius – are a source of endless fascination to a Virgo. They've got so much energy! A Virgo finds an Arien exciting but their relationship could be short-lived because the Virgo will be so irritated by the Arien's devil-may-care attitude to life. When a Virgo pairs up with a Leo, they'll be intrigued by this person's comparatively lavish lifestyle but their own modest temperament will be shocked if the Leo enjoys showing off. A Virgo is able to talk to a Sagittarius until the cows come home – they're both fascinated by ideas, although the precise Virgo will first be amused, and then irritated, by the Sagittarian's rather relaxed attitude to hard facts.

Libra

Of all the members of the zodiac, this is the one that finds it easiest to get on with the other signs. Librans get on particularly well with Geminis and Aquarians, their fellow Air signs. A Libran is enchanted by a Gemini's quick brain and ready wit, and they enjoy endless discussions on all sorts of subjects. When two Librans get together, they revel in the resulting harmonious atmosphere but it's almost impossible for them to reach any decisions – each one defers to the other while being unable to say what they really want. A Libran is intrigued by the independence and sharp mind of an Aquarian, but their feelings could be hurt by the Aquarian's emotional coolness.

Libra enjoys being with the three Fire signs – Aries, Leo and Sagittarius. Libra, who often takes life at rather a slow pace, is energized by a lively Arien, and they complement one another's personalities well. However, the Libran may occasionally feel hurt by the Arien's single-mindedness and blunt speech. A Libran adores the luxury-loving ways of a Leo, and they'll both spend a fortune in the pursuit of happiness. They also get on well in the bedroom. When a Libran gets together with an exuberant Sagittarian, they'll have great fun. All the same, the Sagittarian need for honesty could fluster the Libran, who adopts a much more diplomatic approach to life.

Although the other two Air signs can find it hard to understand members of the Water element, it's different for Librans. They're more sympathetic to the emotional energies of Cancerians, Scorpios and Pisceans. A Libran delights in the protective care of a Cancerian, but those ever-changing Cancerians moods may be hard for a balanced Libran to take. Those deep Scorpio emotions will intrigue the Libran but they may quickly become bogged down by such an intense outlook on life and will be desperate for some light relief. As for Pisces, the Libran is charmed by the Piscean's delicate nature and creative gifts, but both signs hate facing up to unpleasant facts so this couple may never deal with any problems that lie between them.

Libra enjoys the reliable natures of Taurus, Virgo and Capricorn, the Earth signs. A Libran appreciates the company of a relaxed and easy-going Taurean, although they may sometimes regret the Taurean's lack of imagination. When a Libran and a Virgo get together, the Libran enjoys the Virgo's mental abilities but their critical comments will soon cut the Libran to the quick. The Libran may not come back for a second tongue-lashing. A Libran understands the ambitions of a Capricorn, and likes their steady nature and the way they support their family. However, there could soon be rows about money, with the Libran spending a lot more than the Capricorn thinks is necessary.

Scorpio

Not every sign gets on well with its fellow members, yet an astonishing number of Scorpios pair up. They feel safe together because they know the worst and best about each other. When things are good, they're brilliant but these two can also bring out the worst in each other, with intense silences and brooding sulks. A Scorpio enjoys the tender ministrations of a loving Cancerian, and adores being with someone who's so obviously concerned about their welfare. Feelings run deep when a Scorpio pairs up with a Piscean, although the Scorpio may become impatient with the Piscean's reluctance to face up to unpalatable truths.

The three Earth signs, Taurus, Virgo and Capricorn, are well-suited to the Scorpio temperament. Those astrological opposites, Scorpio and Taurus, enjoy a powerful relationship, much of which probably takes place in the bedroom, but whenever they have a disagreement there's an atmosphere you could cut with a knife, and neither of them will be prepared to admit they were in the wrong. A Scorpio is attracted to a neat, analytical Virgo but their feelings will be hurt by this sign's tendency to criticize. What's more, their pride stops them telling the Virgo how they feel. The Scorpio admires a practical Capricorn, especially if they've earned a lot of respect through their work, but this could be a rather chilly pairing because both signs find it difficult to show their feelings.

When you put a Scorpio together with one of the three Fire signs, they'll either get on famously or won't understand one another at all. A Scorpio revels in the lusty Arien's sex drive, although they'll soon feel tired if they try to keep up with the Arien's busy schedule. The combination of Scorpio and Leo packs quite a punch. They're both very strong personalities, but they boss one another around like mad and find it almost impossible to achieve a compromise if they fall out. A Scorpio likes to take life at a measured pace, so they're bemused by a Sagittarian's need to keep busy all the time. In the end, they'll become fed up with never seeing the Sagittarian, or playing second fiddle to all their other interests.

Scorpio is bemused by the three Air signs – Gemini, Libran and Aquarius – because they operate on such completely different wavelengths. A Scorpio can be good friends with a Gemini but they're at emotional cross-purposes, with the Scorpio's intense approach to life too much for a light-hearted Gemini to cope with. Emotions are also the bugbear between a Scorpio and a Libran. Everything is great at first, but the Scorpio's powerful feelings and dark moods will eventually send the Libran running in the opposite direction. You can expect some tense arguments when a Scorpio pairs up with an Aquarian – they're both convinced that they're right and the other one is wrong.

Compatibility in Love and Sex at a glance

F / M	♈	♉	♊	♋	♌	♍	♎	♏	♐	♑	♒	♓
♈	8	5	9	7	9	4	7	8	9	7	7	3
♉	6	8	4	10	7	8	8	7	3	8	2	8
♊	8	2	7	3	8	7	9	4	9	4	9	4
♋	5	10	4	8	6	5	6	8	2	9	2	8
♌	9	8	9	7	7	4	9	6	8	7	9	6
♍	4	8	6	4	4	7	6	7	7	9	4	4
♎	7	8	10	7	8	5	9	6	9	6	10	6
♏	7	9	4	7	6	6	7	10	5	6	5	7
♐	9	4	10	4	9	7	8	4	9	6	9	5
♑	7	8	4	9	6	8	6	4	4	8	4	5
♒	8	6	9	4	9	4	9	6	8	7	8	2
♓	7	6	7	9	6	7	6	9	7	5	4	9

1 = the pits
10 = the peaks

Key

♈ – Aries
♉ – Taurus
♊ – Gemini
♋ – Cancer
♌ – Leo
♍ – Virgo
♎ – Libra
♏ – Scorpio
♐ – Sagittarius
♑ – Capricorn
♒ – Aquarius
♓ – Pisces

Compatibility in Friendship at a glance

M \ F	♈	♉	♊	♋	♌	♍	♎	♏	♐	♑	♒	♓
♈	8	5	10	5	9	3	7	8	9	6	8	5
♉	6	9	6	10	7	8	7	6	4	9	3	9
♊	9	3	9	4	9	8	10	5	10	5	10	6
♋	6	9	4	9	5	4	6	9	4	10	3	9
♌	10	7	9	6	9	4	8	6	9	6	9	7
♍	5	9	8	4	4	8	5	8	8	10	5	6
♎	8	9	10	8	8	6	9	5	9	6	10	7
♏	7	8	5	8	7	7	6	9	4	5	6	8
♐	9	5	10	4	10	8	8	4	10	7	9	6
♑	6	9	5	10	6	9	5	5	4	9	5	6
♒	9	6	10	5	9	5	9	7	9	5	9	3
♓	6	7	6	10	6	8	7	9	8	6	4	10

1 = the pits
10 = the peaks

Key

♈ - Aries
♉ - Taurus
♊ - Gemini
♋ - Cancer
♌ - Leo
♍ - Virgo
♎ - Libra
♏ - Scorpio
♐ - Sagittarius
♑ - Capricorn
♒ - Aquarius
♓ - Pisces

HOBBIES AND THE STARS

What do you do in your spare time? If you're looking for some new interests to keep you occupied in 2000, read on to discover which hobbies are ideal for your Sun sign.

Sagittarius

You're one of the great collectors of the zodiac, whether you know it or not. You may not think that you collect anything at all, but other people will take one look at all your books and beg to disagree with you. Reading is one of your great pleasures in life and you're always buying books on your latest enthusiasms. Travel is something else that appeals to you, and you love planning where you're going to go next on holiday. You like to keep active and you enjoy outdoor sports in particular. Horse-riding is a classic Sagittarian activity, and you enjoy going to the races and having a little flutter. You also like activities that present you with a challenge – you're always determined to beat it!

Capricorn

If you're a typical Capricorn you often take life rather seriously, so it's important for you to have lots of spare-time activities that allow you to relax. However, you've got to find the time first, and that means stopping work rather than burning the candle at both ends. Something that might appeal to you is rock-climbing, and you'll enjoy planning the strategy of how you're going to get to the top. Even a gentle walk amid mountain scenery does you a lot of good and helps you to relax. You're a very practical sign and you enjoy gardening. Not only does it help to ground you, you also like growing your own fruit and vegetables and then comparing the prices with those in the shops. Music helps you to unwind, and you'll love going to the opera or a glittering concert.

Aquarius

Most Aquarians have such a wide range of interests that almost anything is bound to appeal to you. You may go through phases, immersing yourself in one hobby for years until another one takes your fancy. However, you are only interested in activities that keep you intellectually stimulated and that teach you more about the world. You may go to lots of different evening classes, and you might even study for a degree in your spare time. Eastern philosophy could appeal, and you might also be an active campaigner for human rights. Astrology is a big hit with many Aquarians, and you'll enjoy teaching yourself all about it. Group activities are another interest, and you're an avid member of all sorts of organizations and societies.

Pisces

Anything artistic or creative is perfect for you, because you have abundant gifts at your disposal. Painting, drawing, writing poetry and dancing are all classic Piscean pastimes. In fact, you may feel rather fed up or stifled when you can't express yourself creatively. When you want to escape from the world, you love going to the cinema or the theatre. You're a Water sign so you enjoy any activities connected with water, such as swimming or other forms of water sports. Many Pisceans enjoy gardening, and you'll especially like having some form of water feature in your garden even if it's very modest. You're very musical, and would enjoy learning to play an instrument if you can't already do so. You might also like using your psychic talents, perhaps by learning to read the tarot or runes.

Aries

Ariens love to keep active, so you aren't interested in any sort of hobby that's very sedentary or that keeps you glued to the sofa. You much prefer being kept busy, especially if it's out of doors. You also have a strong sense of adventure and a great love of speed, so one hobby that's right up your street is motor-racing. You might be lucky enough to be the driver, or you could be a spectator shouting yourself hoarse from the stands, but this is a sport you love. Speaking of sports, anything that's competitive and which threatens to knock the stuffing out of you will also suit you down to the ground. Rugby, football and baseball all fit the bill, and you might also enjoy martial arts and Eastern forms of exercise such as T'ai Chi.

Taurus

You belong to one of the Earth signs, so it's no surprise that many Taureans were born with green fingers. You always feel better when you can be out in the fresh air, especially if you're in beautiful surroundings, so you adore gardening. Even if you're not keen on wielding a spade yourself you'll enjoy appreciating other people's efforts. Cooking is something that has enormous appeal for you and you enjoy creating gourmet meals, especially if the ingredients include your favourite foods. You also enjoy visiting swanky restaurants, although some of the gilt will be wiped off the gingerbread if you don't think you're getting value for money. Members of your sign are renowned for having beautiful voices so you might enjoy singing in a choir or on your own.

Gemini

One of your favourite ways of passing the time is to curl up with a good book. You'll eagerly read newspapers and magazines as well, and you always attempt crosswords and other sorts of puzzle even if you don't always finish them. Jigsaws intrigue you, especially if you can do something else at the same time, such as listening to music or watching the TV. You belong to a sign that doesn't like sitting still for long and you absolutely thrive on keeping active, so it's important for you to enjoy hobbies that make sure you get plenty of exercise. Tennis is a classic Gemini sport because it involves a lot of skill but it also boosts your social life. Dancing is another activity that helps you to keep fit while having a really good time.

Cancer

Home comforts are very important to you, so you spend a lot of time and money on making sure your home is the way you want it. You may enjoy reading magazines on interior design or you could be glued to all the DIY programmes on TV, adapting the best ideas for your own home. One of your greatest skills is cooking, because you belong to a sign that derives enormous emotional comfort from food. You take pleasure in cooking for your loved ones and you probably have a big collection of cookery books to provide you with endless inspiration. Water sports could appeal to you, especially if they involve visiting your favourite beach. You might also enjoy fishing, particularly if you can do it by moonlight.

Leo

You have a host of artistic skills and talents at your fingertips because you belong to the one of the most creative signs in the zodiac. One of your favourite hobbies is amateur dramatics, because most Leos adore being in the limelight. You may even have thought about becoming a professional actor because you enjoy treading the boards so much. You might also enjoy dancing, whether you go to regular classes or you simply love tripping the light fantastic with your partner. Travel appeals to you, especially if you can visit luxurious hotels in hot parts of the world. However, you're not very keen on roughing it! Clothes are very important to you, so you enjoy shopping for the latest fashions and you may also be an accomplished dressmaker.

Virgo

One of your favourite pastimes is to keep up to date with your health. You're fascinated by medical matters and you enjoy reading books telling you how to keep fit. You may even try out all the latest eating regimes, hoping that you'll find one that suits you perfectly. This interest in health means you're keen to eat well, and you could enjoy growing your own vegetables. Even cultivating a few herbs in a windowbox will give you a sense of achievement and you'll be pleased to think they are doing you good. You have tremendous patience so you might enjoy fiddly hobbies that require great dexterity, such as knitting, needlepoint and sewing. You might also enjoy painting designs on china and glass.

Libra

Libra is a very sensual sign, so any hobbies that appeal to your senses are bound to go down well. You love delicious smells so you might enjoy learning about aromatherapy, so you can cure yourself of minor ailments and also create your own bath oils. You could also get a big thrill out of making your own cosmetics or soaps, and you might become so good at them that you give them away as gifts. You take great pride in looking good, so you enjoy visiting your favourite shops and keeping up with the latest fashions. Music is one of your great loves and you might play an instrument or sing. If not, you certainly appreciate other people's musical talents and you enjoy going to concerts and recitals.

Scorpio

Whatever hobbies you choose, they have to mean a lot to you. You simply aren't interested in activities that don't carry an emotional meaning for you and you'd rather not bother with them at all. One pastime that's dear to the hearts of most Scorpios is wine-tasting. You might enjoy teaching yourself all about wine, either with the help of some good books or simply by drinking whatever appeals to you. You're fascinated by mysteries, and you could enjoy reading lots of whodunits or books on true crimes. You are also intrigued by things that go bump in the night, and you can't resist going on ghost hunts or visiting famous places that are known to be haunted.

THE YEAR 2000

Friends and Lovers

You start the year on great form. No wonder, because your loving relationships flourished in 1999 and this happy trend continues into the first six weeks of 2000. It's the ideal time to enjoy the company of other people and to make sure your social life is living up to expectations. If you're a single Sagittarian at the start of the year, you've got six weeks to change all that and find someone who really brightens up your life.

It isn't only your love life that will benefit at the start of the year. You'll find it easy to get on well with all your loved ones, whether you're linked by passion, friendship or blood ties.

One-to-one relationships will blossom from June onwards, when it's a marvellous time to join forces with other people. It's the ideal opportunity to pledge your troth or move in with someone, and you may even embark on a new relationship in which everything happens really fast. Yes, you could be swept off your feet!

Even so, 2000 could be a testing time for relationships that aren't going as well as you'd like. Any liaison that has reached the end of the road or which is no longer right for you will start to show the cracks. It may even come to an end, in which case you can comfort yourself with the knowledge that another relationship will come along in its place before too long.

Relationships with close relatives, neighbours and people that you see on a regular basis could also go through some changes this year. You might see a new side to someone's character or you could make a whole new set of acquaintances. Try not to take anyone for granted or to judge them by appearances because, if you do, you could be in for a big surprise. By the way, if you would like to increase your social circle, a good way to do this is to become involved in local activities and community projects. You could meet some very interesting people as a result.

Health

Good news! You're blessed with a lot of energy and vitality this year, and it will be especially noticeable between February and June. During this time you'll enjoy doing things that keep you fighting fit and which boost your well-being. It's a marvellous chance to take up a new sport or to find a form of exercise that is so enjoyable you don't mind doing it several times a week. However, you won't always have a lot of willpower and so you'll find it hard to resist eating and drinking to your heart's content. As a result, you could start to pile on the pounds. Try not to go overboard too often, especially if you suffer from the classic Sagittarian problem of feeling liverish when you overdo the rich food and fine wines. Rather than limit yourself to a strict diet of lettuce leaves and carrot juice, you'll do far better if you eat healthy but delicious food.

You'll be kept very busy this year so it's important for you to recharge your batteries whenever you get the chance. Try to make sure you get plenty of rest and relaxation, especially if you're worried about something or you've been burning the candle at both ends. Investigate any strange ailments that don't want to go away because otherwise you'll start to worry about them. You should also keep active, partly because this will help you to feel fit but also because it will keep your joints supple and in good condition.

With Pluto currently moving through your own sign of Sagittarius, you're going through a period of major transformation. This means that your life is changing for the better, although it may not feel like that at the time. If you're finding life very stressful or upsetting, make sure you take good care of yourself. You might find it beneficial to read some self-help books or to practise creative visualization, so you feel you've got some control over what's happening to you.

Money

With so many changes taking place in your life at the moment, your finances are bound to be affected. This is especially likely if you were born between 2 and 8 December, and you may be struggling to maintain your customary optimism. But don't worry because you will win through in the end, even though it may be hard going at the time. Try to set aside some money for a rainy day, so you've got it for emergencies. It's certainly not a good idea to overcommit yourself financially at the moment because, even though you may scrape together the money to pay your debts, you could find the stress of it all is too much for you. It will be better to keep within your financial limits whenever possible.

Take care during the first six weeks of the year because this could be a very expensive time for you. Your social life really blossoms until the middle of February, and as a result it could make a big dent in your finances. However, if you've got the money to spare, this is the ideal time to buy things that will improve your image or make you feel good. So you've got every excuse to go mad in the sales, to treat yourself to lots of new clothes or to have a complete make-over.

If you're fed up with your current job because it isn't paying enough money, you could receive a rise or some perks between February and June. Alternatively, this is when you should make a concerted effort to find another job.

Pay particular attention to your finances in January, between June and July, and also in December. These are all months in which you should make sure your money matters are up to date. They are also excellent times to make some investments for the future or to make some major purchases.

Career

You start the year in great form, and you'll really enjoy doing things that bring out your creative talents. You may be lucky enough to do this as part of your job or you could be invited to do something that acts as a showcase for some of your abilities. One thing is for sure – you should grab every chance to express your talents and skills in the first six weeks of the year, because you don't know where they'll lead you.

You'll be kept really busy between January and August. You may be asked to do some extra work or you could be given more responsibility in your current job. Alternatively, you might land a new job that will keep you on your toes. Although you won't get the chance to coast along or take things easy, you will be given the opportunity to prove yourself and to show that you're a valuable person to have around. So if you want to impress your workmates or climb another rung up the ladder of success, this is the time to do it!

Colleagues and clients will be fun to be around this year, especially between February and June, and you'll enjoy their company. You might even find that a workmate does you a favour or gives you a fantastic opportunity. If you're fed up with your current job, this is the time to look for something new. You could find just the thing you were looking for!

Many areas of your life are currently undergoing a fundamental transformation, and your career may be one of them. If so, you may be feeling dissatisfied with your current profession and wondering what to do instead. You may yearn to do something that has more meaning for you or that puts your talents to good use. But don't be surprised if your career takes off in a completely different direction to the one it's heading in at the moment. Some massive changes are coming your way!

Your Day by Day Guide

JANUARY AT A GLANCE

Love	♥ ♥ ♥
Money	£ $ £ $ £
Career	💻 💻
Health	☼ ☼

• *Saturday 1 January* •

Happy New Year! It looks as though you're all set to start afresh and make some very positive changes in the coming days and weeks. If you're a true Sagittarian, you're at your happiest when you're making plans for the future, and you're feeling so confident and optimistic today that you're likely to be thinking big. If you start as you mean to go on, there'll be no stopping you in 2000!

• *Sunday 2 January* •

This is a wonderful day to catch up with old friends and simply enjoy each other's company. You're feeling at your most generous and receptive, and everyone who comes into your orbit today is likely to feel uplifted by your presence. In fact, you'll be the life and soul of any party you go to. Any new people that you meet now could well become very significant in the future.

• *Monday 3 January* •

If you have to go back to work today you'll feel as if you've come down to earth with a bump. Adapting to any routine won't be easy because you're much more in the mood to dream about your next holiday or weekend away. Try to ease yourself back into routine gently by choosing a task that doesn't require prolonged concentration and which you can do without too much effort.

• *Tuesday 4 January* •

You've still got your head in the clouds, which makes it difficult to reach any decisions that require clear thinking. Your imagination is running riot, with new ideas and exciting projects that you hope to put into action. Anything or anyone that threatens to burst your enthusiastic bubble is likely to get their head bitten off. Give yourself time to feel more grounded.

• *Wednesday 5 January* •

Being a Sagittarian, you are sure to value your freedom very highly. Today is one of those days when you feel a particularly strong need to assert your independence and do your own thing. If you get the chance to do this, you'll get a lot done as there's nothing to hold you back and you can fire on all cylinders. If you do need to cooperate with others, encourage them to be as self-reliant as possible.

• *Thursday 6 January* •

The more you put into your life today the more you'll get back. You can lay some very positive foundations for the year ahead just by setting your objectives and having a very clear intention of what it is you want to achieve. The dreamy state you were in at the beginning of the week has given way to a much more resolute frame of mind, and you're ready for action.

• *Friday 7 January* •

You probably won't want to be bothered today by any annoying minor details that need sorting out. The trouble is that if you want your plans to be successful and to get off the ground, you have no choice but to tackle any potential problems that could jeopardize the smooth running of things. It's a question of gritting your teeth and getting on with it.

• *Saturday 8 January* •

All your relationships, whether personal or professional, get a much needed boost today. Knowing that you can count on everyone's support gives you the extra confidence to ask for the resources you need to translate a dream into reality. One way or another, you are likely to be lucky financially and you could even have an unexpected windfall. Perfect timing!

• *Sunday 9 January* •

Your mind has been elsewhere recently and as a result you might be caught off guard today by someone who has designs on you. The attraction between the two of you could prove to be irresistible and you may feel compelled to act out a strong desire to deepen your connection with this person. This could create a lot of negative emotions, such as guilt, if you're already in a relationship. Proceed with caution.

• *Monday 10 January* •

Say what you mean and mean what you say today, otherwise you could end up with a misunderstanding that's hard to clear up. If you're not afraid to voice your feelings and speak the truth, you should be able to avoid a difficult situation with a partner or loved one. Trying to cover up how you really feel is much more likely to provoke an argument than being honest.

• *Tuesday 11 January* •

You won't be able to get away with deluding yourself or others today, so try to be as aware of yourself and your motivations as possible. You could be acting on an impulse that you don't fully understand and, unless you want all hell to break loose, it's important that you get to grips with your motives. Be prepared to face up to your feelings rather than pretend to ignore them.

• *Wednesday 12 January* •

Your boredom threshold is at an all-time low today so make sure you seek out stimulating company and do things that challenge and stretch you. The tried and tested path is not one to take in your present mood because you'll only end up feeling stifled and irritated. The unknown may be full of surprises but, for your adventurous spirit, that can only be a bonus now.

• *Thursday 13 January* •

Objectivity and reason seem to have temporarily deserted you and your emotions are stronger and more powerful than usual. You approach everything you do today with great passion and feeling, and you could even find yourself getting obsessed about something or someone. Although this could totally dominate your thinking for a short but intense period, the after-effects will last a long time.

• *Friday 14 January* •

It looks as if a few home truths are heading in your direction from a disgruntled partner or close friend. You may not like what you hear but at least it will break the tension that's been building up between you. So much of what you think and feel is in a state of flux at the moment and it's better to admit this rather than pretend to be something you're not.

• *Saturday 15 January* •

You're determined to speak your mind today but it might be more productive if you view it as getting your point of view across instead. If you present yourself too forcefully, you'll only antagonize the people you're seeking to be on good terms with. You'll score far more points if you can resist the temptation to impose your version of reality on the situation.

• *Sunday 16 January* •

Patience may not be your strong suit but that's exactly what you need in order to get an important job done today. Sustaining your interest in a task that doesn't challenge you or teach you something is difficult to say the least, but this could prove to be a very valuable experience. See it as a learning curve and you could change your whole attitude as a result.

• *Monday 17 January* •

Throwing caution to the winds? You're in your element today, and provided you don't take on more than you can handle, you can get ahead in almost anything you set your sights on. Something that you've wanted to do for a long time but which felt too daunting now seems within reach, and you're willing to take the risk involved in making it happen.

• *Tuesday 18 January* •

Today's planetary set-up offers an ideal opportunity to clear the air and release any hidden tensions between you and a loved one. It may not be easy to say sorry, but if an apology is due it could go a long way towards healing any resentments that have accumulated over time. You'll feel so much better afterwards that you'll wonder why you didn't do it sooner. Oh well, we all live and learn!

• *Wednesday 19 January* •

You could be expecting far too much of yourself today. That means you may be setting yourself up to fail and feel bad about yourself when you don't live up to your own high standards. If you can be a little more realistic about what you're capable of, instead of exaggerating your abilities, you're much more likely to succeed and not lose face.

• *Thursday 20 January* •

If you feel as if you're on a different planet from everyone else today it's probably because you're trying to communicate something that nobody can really understand. The most likely reason for this is that you are still unclear in your own mind about what it is you want to say. Once the fog clears you'll know exactly how to put your feelings across. In the meantime, be patient.

• *Friday 21 January* •

Although you're much more clear-headed today, you still haven't sorted out the difference between your emotions and what your logical side is telling you. If you feel torn over an emotional issue, you might need some input to help resolve the split between the two sides of you. Why not talk to someone who is completely impartial and can act as a sounding board?

• *Saturday 22 January* •

You could be in store for a big surprise today on the relationship front. Either you'll be dropping a bombshell or your partner will be making an unexpected announcement. Either way, it seems a change is inevitable and, even though it may shake up the status quo, at least you won't be able to complain that you're bored and that life is uneventful. It's quite the reverse today!

• *Sunday 23 January* •

Today's a great day to tackle anything that you've been putting off or avoiding in the hope that it'll simply go away. What you now realize is that things will only get worse if you bury your head in the sand and, unless you act now, they could get completely out of hand. At least you've found the courage and determination to sort things out, even if you don't relish the idea of doing it.

• *Monday 24 January* •

You're able to put yourself in somebody else's shoes today and see things from their perspective. As a result, you feel more than willing to compromise and not push so hard for what you want. In fact, you may even decide that what you once felt so strongly about is no longer worth fighting for and that it makes more sense to follow another path.

• *Tuesday 25 January* •

You should be able to enjoy a stress-free day today and let go of any worrying thoughts that have been occupying your mind recently. One way to lift your spirits would be to spend some time with people who like you just the way you are, so you don't have to pretend to be something you're not. You're probably more in the mood for being at home and having open house and, if you're a typical Sagittarian, you'll be entertaining on a grand scale now.

• *Wednesday 26 January* •

Your perception is much sharper than usual and you're able to read between the lines of a statement that a close friend or relative makes. The question is whether you let on that you know what they're really thinking, or you keep quiet and play the game. If you can get to the bottom of why they're being so secretive, you'll be in a better position to decide what's going on.

• *Thursday 27 January* •

In spite of the fact that you're feeling quite buoyant and happy, the day isn't without its challenges. Your good-natured mood could be tested by someone at work who tries to coerce you into doing something you don't really want to do. Although the last thing you want is to make an issue over it, they probably won't give up until you make a stand.

• *Friday 28 January* •

If you could shut out the rest of the world today and have the whole day to yourself, that's probably exactly what you would like to do. You need some time alone to take stock of how you're feeling and what you need for yourself. Although you may not be able to isolate yourself completely, at least give yourself some space to gather your thoughts and consider your next move.

• *Saturday 29 January* •

Yesterday's introspective mood already seems like history as you begin to sense a new and exciting wind of change blowing through your life. Your normal intuition is heightened and the insights you gain today could be the catalyst for a major turning point. Keep an open mind and don't be afraid to experiment with new ideas.

• *Sunday 30 January* •

Somebody may be trying to clip your wings today. Could it be that they're feeling threatened by your growing restlessness? In any case, this person's attitude does have the effect of dampening your enthusiasm and draining your energy. What transpires today will show you one way or another whether your need for greater freedom is compatible with those around you.

• *Monday 31 January* •

You can make some far-reaching changes today without burning your bridges and disrupting the positive elements of your life. You always benefit enormously from seeing the bigger picture and finding a meaning to whatever you are experiencing. And today you have the courage of your convictions if you want to strike a blow for freedom and still keep your feet on the ground.

FEBRUARY AT A GLANCE

Love	♥ ♥
Money	£ $
Career	💻 💻 💻
Health	☼ ☼ ☼

• *Tuesday 1 February* •

This is an ideal day to have a good clear-out at home of any clutter that you've been meaning to get rid of but never got round to. You'll be amazed at how much more space you have once you've lightened the load of accumulated possessions that you no longer have a use for. You'll feel a lot freer, both physically and psychologically.

• *Wednesday 2 February* •

You may have to face up to the fact that you're only human, and when you set yourself unrealistic goals you end up feeling extremely disillusioned. There are certain obligations that you have to live up to and these take priority today over any future aspirations you would like to fulfil. So rather than get carried away, focus on the here and now.

• *Thursday 3 February* •

Even though your customary honesty and directness can occasionally put people's backs up, you're able to tell others exactly where you stand today without unduly offending anyone. In fact, because you're able to be so straight and open in the way you communicate, you will earn the respect and admiration of those who prefer the direct approach.

• *Friday 4 February* •

If you have to negotiate any contracts today, you'll have the skill and ability to make sure everyone feels satisfied that they've got the best deal possible. This is partly because you're simply not aware of what it is that you want, but it is also because you are currently feeling sympathetic to everyone else's wishes. This puts you in a strong position to smooth over what could have been a very bumpy ride.

• *Saturday 5 February* •

Everything feels in a state of flux today and in many ways this signifies the opportunity to make a new start in your personal life. You could become very aware of how a part of you has been functioning on auto-pilot for a while, and the reasons why you have felt like this may well come to light. Talking things through will help you to get them into perspective.

• *Sunday 6 February* •

You could be in store for a few more stark realizations today. These can only serve to strengthen your resolve to change some old and outworn patterns. Your worst nightmare is to settle down into a dreary, lifeless routine so, to prevent that happening, you need to inject your life with new energy. As long as you aren't too rash, you can initiate some very positive changes now.

• *Monday 7 February* •

You're probably still reeling from the whirlwind events of the weekend and need a quiet, low-key day to catch your breath. There's still a lot to sort out and in many ways you now have to restructure your life in order to accommodate what is new. If you feel more sombre and serious today about what's transpired recently, give some room to these feelings rather than dismiss them as negative.

• *Tuesday 8 February* •

Conserve your energies today and only do what's absolutely necessary. You're probably emotionally and physically drained and simply don't have the stamina to go charging about in your normal fashion. Pacing yourself will give you the time to recover and then, before you know it, you'll be chomping at the bit again and ready to get back into the swing of things.

• *Wednesday 9 February* •

Be careful that you don't get so wrapped up in your own emotions today that you are oblivious to how other people are feeling. It's not that you're being selfish deliberately, it's just that you are more in touch with your emotional state than usual. If you extend this sensitivity to a partner or loved one, you could have the perfect recipe for romance.

• *Thursday 10 February* •

You're feeling very protective towards your loved ones today and you might want to spend more time than usual letting them know how much you really care. If you're true to your Sun sign you never become extremely possessive, but you realize now just how attached you are to your nearest and dearest and how important it is to acknowledge your feelings for them.

• *Friday 11 February* •

It's a great day to cast a much-needed critical eye over a problem in your home that needs to be fixed. You may need to call in expert help, even if it is expensive, but your main concern is to repair the damage before it becomes a bigger headache than it is already. And while you're at it, see if you need to do any other jobs that you've been turning a blind eye to.

• *Saturday 12 February* •

Your normal routine is disrupted today by an unexpected call from someone from the past, especially if they are an old flame or you once held a torch for them. This could spark off all kinds of explosive emotions but try not to do anything rash and impulsive that you could regret later on. Either way, the situation looks extremely volatile and ideally you should keep a low profile until you can control your unpredictable behaviour.

• *Sunday 13 February* •

Your love life looks more like a smoking fuse than a bed of roses today, and you really need to take the initiative and restore the peace. Whatever you do, don't make the mistake of leading anyone on or giving them the wrong message. You know in your heart where your loyalties lie, and once you've made that perfectly obvious to everyone concerned, any confusion will be cleared up once and for all.

• *Monday 14 February* •

Happy Valentine's Day! It's an ideal time to offer the olive branch and get your relationship with a certain someone back on track. There could be some very deep and intense exchanges between you and your loved one, and the more you can bare your souls the closer you will feel to one another. There's a powerful attraction between you and this promises to be a day to remember.

• *Tuesday 15 February* •

There doesn't seem to be a cloud in the sky today and you can relax in the knowledge that all's well in your world. You're feeling at your most sociable, and even if you have a job to do you would rather work as part of a team than by yourself. Any group activity will go well today, and there's a lot to be gained from pooling your resources with others.

• *Wednesday 16 February* •

If you're a true Sagittarian, you have a great thirst for knowledge and today you may learn something that stimulates your curiosity about the world. You might want to investigate a new subject that you know nothing about, or perhaps you could find out something fascinating about your family history. You're about to embark on a journey of discovery!

• *Thursday 17 February* •

'Live now pay later' could easily be your motto today, but you may have to curb your desire to be extravagant or you could end up out of pocket. You're really in the mood to indulge yourself and you need to do something out of the ordinary that makes you feel special. You're also feeling very magnanimous, and whoever you're with will be given the star treatment.

• *Friday 18 February* •

The coming fortnight is an ideal time to get one step closer towards realizing those all important goals you've set for yourself. However, be prepared to make some adjustments before you can forge full steam ahead. For instance, you may have to change your original course of action but this will probably work out to your advantage in the long run. You've got your sights set on success!

• *Saturday 19 February* •

Home and domestic matters will play a major part in your life over the coming month. You might start thinking about moving house or you could ponder ways of improving your current set-up. Perhaps it's about time you did some decorating? Don't be surprised if your thoughts start straying to the past or you spend a lot of time wallowing in nostalgic day-dreams.

• *Sunday 20 February* •

You'd like nothing better today than simply to follow your trains of thought and see where they lead but, unfortunately, there are more pressing issues to deal with. Certain duties or responsibilities that you agreed to take on need your full attention now and, even though you feel restricted by these demands, at least you've got the good grace to rise to the occasion.

• *Monday 21 February* •

You feel quite content in your everyday surroundings today and have no great wish to travel very far afield. In fact, you could be viewing your immediate environment with fresh eyes and appreciating all the good things around you. It's a great opportunity to get to know someone that you see on a regular basis but who is still a bit of a stranger, such as a neighbour or workmate.

• *Tuesday 22 February* •

Any unresolved tension between you and a colleague could lead to a full-blown confrontation today. If you feel legitimate anger over something it's probably better not to bottle it up but, by the same token, be wary of getting into an argument just for the sake of it. Air your grievances by all means, but try to come to a resolution and then put the whole thing behind you.

• *Wednesday 23 February* •

It's a question of give and take today if things are to run smoothly and without any hiccups. There's a lot of activity around you, and you may be asked to take charge of a group or to coordinate a project that requires total cooperation from everyone concerned. Your energy and enthusiasm are contagious and you'll soon have everyone pulling together.

• *Thursday 24 February* •

Someone that you thought you could count on may well prove to be somewhat elusive today, and you might end up asking yourself if your trust was misplaced. You probably like to believe the best about people and, although you're often right in your judgements, you can occasionally delude yourself. If that is what has happened in this case, try to see it positively. What can you learn from the experience?

• *Friday 25 February* •

You could set the cat among the pigeons today with an outspoken remark or some unusual behaviour. You may just feel like having a laugh but, if it's at someone else's expense, it could backfire on you and get you into trouble. It's probably wise to make sure that whoever you decide to have some fun with has a sense of humour. Otherwise, you may have to do some fast-talking to get yourself out of trouble!

• *Saturday 26 February* •

The sparks of passion between you and a special someone are about to ignite, and it looks as though you're all set for an amorous weekend. If you can get away and have some time alone, then so much the better – the last thing you want is to have your everyday life intrude on your time together. Whether you're at home or away, the stage is set for a romantic and magical interlude.

• *Sunday 27 February* •

There are no holds barred today when it comes to emotional matters, and you might even surprise yourself by how strongly you feel about certain subjects. You're certainly not in the mood to play games with anyone's feelings and you don't want there to be any doubt about what's in your heart. Not that you could hide your feelings in any case – you may be wearing your heart on your sleeve.

• *Monday 28 February* •

You've got a one-track mind today and anybody who tries to engage you in conversation will be wasting their time! What took place over the weekend has knocked you for six and you really can't think of anything else. The only difficulty that this could create is if you have to present a balanced, rational face to the world. If so, forget it!

• *Tuesday 29 February* •

Take care today because you could be feeling very rash and impulsive, ready to make all sorts of drastic changes to your life without really thinking them through. Although there may well be things that need changing, think twice before you act prematurely. Why not make a list of your plans, and then give yourself a few days to decide if they are still valid? At least that will stop you throwing out the baby with the bathwater.

MARCH AT A GLANCE

Love	♥ ♥ ♥ ♥ ♥
Money	£
Career	💻 💻 💻 💻
Health	☼ ☼ ☼ ☼

• *Wednesday 1 March* •

You won't want to do anything by half measures today and you're ready to throw yourself wholeheartedly into a new project or experience. This energetic approach will make you a winner because other people will be charmed and fascinated by your dare-devil attitude. And even though this doesn't always create the desired result, this time it looks as though it might pay off.

• *Thursday 2 March* •

Ready to put your money where your mouth is? Make sure you really do have the courage of your convictions today, because if you say something without meaning it you could lose a lot of credibility. Organize your ideas so that everything you say makes sense and is taken seriously. It really won't help if people take what you say with a pinch of salt. This is especially important if you're talking to someone connected with your work or health.

• *Friday 3 March* •

You could be given the cold shoulder by a relative or neighbour today, in which case you'll wonder what on earth you did to deserve it. It probably won't do much good to try to break the ice because this person is obviously not in the mood to be humoured right now. Give them a few days to come round, and then with luck they'll be willing to talk things through.

• *Saturday 4 March* •

If yesterday's events have left you feeling misunderstood and confused, don't let these feelings build up. Instead, do something positive so you can take your mind off it. Otherwise, you could get yourself into such a state that you make the situation worse by adding fuel to the fire. Spend some time with people whose company you always enjoy.

• *Sunday 5 March* •

You fancy spending some time at home today and recharging your batteries. You need to give yourself a complete day of rest and, in order to do that, you may have to be very firm with any family and friends who have other plans for you. With a bit of luck they'll finally get the message and leave you to enjoy a wonderfully lazy and indulgent day.

• *Monday 6 March* •

Whatever projects you start today will have important repercussions in the weeks to come. If you're thinking about moving house or doing some home improvements, this is an ideal time to get the ball rolling. Even if all you end up doing is blowing away the cobwebs by doing some spring cleaning, the effect will be wonderfully uplifting. The coming fortnight is also a marvellous chance to make a fresh start with someone close to your heart.

• *Tuesday 7 March* •

You're in a dream world today and your imagination is running riot, especially if you are thinking about all the places you'd love to visit. If you're a typical Sagittarius you love to travel, especially if it's somewhere off the beaten track. Why not take yourself off to a travel agent and choose one of those exotic destinations for your next holiday? Failing that, a change of scene will give you plenty to think about.

• *Wednesday 8 March* •

A close friend might confide in you today and ask you to help them to resolve a difficult situation. You may feel that they've been unfairly treated, in which case you will be extra keen to lend a hand. Your innate sense of fairness is something you strongly believe in and you're willing to fight to see justice done. No doubt this is why your friend turned to you in the first place.

• *Thursday 9 March* •

You could charm the birds off the trees today! As a result, everything will happen with incredible ease. Sagittarians are often blessed with a terrific sense of humour and you really are able to laugh at yourself, which is one of the characteristics that most endears you to other people. Your good mood is contagious and anyone who spends time with you today will feel a whole lot better for it.

• *Friday 10 March* •

Certain work-related matters need urgent attention today, and you'll have to be as disciplined as possible in order to get the job done in the limited time available. Planning your day in advance will give you a head start and, provided you don't lose your momentum halfway through, you should gain a great deal of satisfaction from what you achieve.

• *Saturday 11 March* •

Have a look in the mirror. Are you thinking about changing your appearance in some way and finding a new image? If so, this is a marvellous day to make a start. How about looking around your favourite clothes shops or having your hair cut in a new style? Of course, you could have more innovative ideas that you are longing to try out. Either way, you'll have a lot of fun now!

• *Sunday 12 March* •

The higher your expectations are today, the more likely you are to be disappointed when life fails to come up to scratch. That is especially likely if you have high hopes of a certain person. Are they always reliable or have they let you down in the past? If so, they could let you down again today, or perhaps you wish they could be something that they're not? Try to be realistic about other people's foibles and failings because that will reduce your chances of being disappointed by them.

• *Monday 13 March* •

Be careful when talking to a loved one today. You could easily end up at talking at cross-purposes with them, because what starts off as a genuine misunderstanding could soon snowball into a major disagreement. If things do become emotionally stormy, try to find what caused the upset in the first place. It could be that you're making a mountain out of a molehill.

• *Tuesday 14 March* •

You can find a very creative solution to any problem that you face today and, with a bit of luck, everyone concerned will be only too pleased to accept what you propose. Once you've put this problem behind you, try to spend at least part of the day doing something that inspires and uplifts you. You're particularly sensitive to beauty today, so go somewhere that's easy on the eye.

• *Wednesday 15 March* •

Your competitive instinct is aroused today and you're determined to go for gold. You may well have to pit your wits against some stiff competition, but the challenge will only serve to strengthen your resolve. You've been waiting for an opportunity to prove yourself and it now looks as though the world is about to see what you're really made of.

• *Thursday 16 March* •

Just when you thought you could see the bigger picture and knew exactly where you were going, something comes along to blur the edges today. Part of the confusion lies in the fact that you may have jumped to conclusions before you had the whole story, and you're now discovering that what you thought was fact is really wishful thinking. Wait until you've got a handle on the truth before you act.

• *Friday 17 March* •

You feel extraordinarily flirtatious today! If you've got your eye on a certain person, they will certainly notice you now. If you want to know how they feel about you, this is a good day to make a play for them. If there's only a lukewarm response, you'll probably conclude that you're wasting your time. If, however, they take the bait, you won't hold back from putting your powers of seduction to the test.

• *Saturday 18 March* •

You're not keen to work or play hard today and will much prefer ease and comfort to strenuous activity. Even if you simply put your feet up and relax with a good book, you'll feel pleased with yourself and give yourself a much-needed day off. The best part of it is that you know you deserve this break, so you don't have to feel even remotely guilty.

• *Sunday 19 March* •

You've got renewed energy today, but if you're not careful you could go into overdrive and forget all about your good intentions to take it easy. Not only that, you might decide you want to get everyone else involved in a major activity and end up with a lot of disgruntled people who are in no mood to be organized. Pace yourself because then life will be a lot easier.

• *Monday 20 March* •

Although by nature you probably tend to look on the bright side, you're feeling uncharacteristically gloomy today and lacking in your normal optimism. What's more, you tend to be rather harsh on yourself and unnecessarily self-critical. If you're really honest with yourself, you may come up with a few home truths, but surely nothing to warrant such despondency.

• *Tuesday 21 March* •

If you're involved in any sort of group activities today you'll certainly stand out as someone who has something to say. At the risk of being unpopular, you will dare to speak your truth and not pull your punches. Even so, you will still be able to listen to what others have to say, and this will go down very well with a certain person.

• *Wednesday 22 March* •

A family member will be very helpful today, especially if they can assist you in coming to terms with a problem you've been wrestling with for a while. Not only does this person have a special insight into what makes you tick, they also have a great deal of affection for you. You wouldn't confide in just anyone, but you know you can trust this person implicitly.

• *Thursday 23 March* •

You've got plenty to mull over today concerning how emotionally secure you are feeling at the moment. So be honest with yourself. Is everything OK or are you unsure where you stand with a certain someone? Perhaps you feel as though the rug has been pulled out from under you and you don't know where you stand. In reality, this may be more to do with your own feelings of insecurity rather than a lack of commitment from the other person. Only time will tell.

• *Friday 24 March* •

You're so tuned into everyone's emotions today that you feel more like a psychic sponge than a person! The positive side of this means that you can relate very sensitively to those around you and will instinctively know what they need. However, you may also feel swamped by other people's emotions, which can be exhausting. You may want to give a wide berth to anyone who is miserable or depressed at the best of times.

• *Saturday 25 March* •

Even though you are more open-minded than most, you will still find it a struggle today to put any preconceived thoughts to one side and look at something from an entirely new perspective. If it has been difficult to resolve a problem connected with your home or work, you may need to adopt a new tactic in order to achieve a better understanding with everyone concerned.

• *Sunday 26 March* •

This is one of those wonderful days when you can count your blessings and feel happy with your lot. You value the friends that you have, especially the long-lasting ones that have stood the test of time. One particular friendship that has proven to be particularly enduring and reliable comes up trumps again today. Don't forget to let this person know how much you appreciate them!

• *Monday 27 March* •

Are you ready to splash out? Your finances receive a boost today, which gives you the confidence to go ahead and buy something you've had your eye on for some time, especially if you couldn't afford it until now. You're in the mood to shop until you drop but keep an eye on how much you spend, otherwise you could get carried away and end up in worse financial shape than before.

• *Tuesday 28 March* •

If you were able to restrain yourself yesterday financially, you're probably feeling very pleased with yourself. Not only have you indulged your spending urge, you've also managed to keep your bank balance in a healthy state. At the moment it's important for you to feel financially secure, mainly because you know it gives you more flexibility and a greater freedom of choice in what you do.

• *Wednesday 29 March* •

Be careful that you don't try to bulldoze someone into agreeing with you today. Even though you may feel passionately about something, and you want everyone else to have the same conviction, you will have accept the fact that not everyone does. Forcing your beliefs on certain individuals isn't going win them over! Try a more subtle approach, and if they don't take the bait, leave it at that.

• *Thursday 30 March* •

You long to get away from your immediate environment today and spend some time in quiet, beautiful surroundings. You're in a reflective, dreamy mood and you feel like letting yourself drift for a while. Anyone who spends any time with you today will find you somewhat vague and detached. What you really need is a Do Not Disturb sign around your neck!

• *Friday 31 March* •

If you've recently moved into a new neighbourhood, this is an ideal opportunity to have a social evening and get to know your new neighbours. Even if you've been living in your present home for a while, it still wouldn't go amiss to arrange a get-together for your friends and neighbours. You might be surprised to find how many kindred spirits are literally round the corner!

APRIL AT A GLANCE

Love	♥ ♥ ♥ ♥ ♥
Money	£
Career	💻 💻 💻 💻 💻
Health	☼ ☼ ☼ ☼ ☼

• *Saturday 1 April* •

You are blessed with some extra sparkle today and, without any effort on your part, you'll positively dazzle everyone you come into contact with. If you have been admiring someone from afar, now is the time to move in closer and knock them for six. Unless they're wearing a suit of armour, there's no way they can defend themselves against the kind of impact you're making.

• *Sunday 2 April* •

If you have already set aside today to do some jobs around the home, you will be better off sticking to your plans rather than trying to find a let-out clause. That is because you currently have the discipline to apply yourself to even the most boring or dreary tasks, so you might as well get them out of the way while you are in the mood. Think how pleased with yourself you will feel when they're all done!

• *Monday 3 April* •

If you're a true-to-type Sagittarian, you don't like to be tied down and you prefer a job where you can have as much autonomy as possible. If you don't have that kind of freedom in your current situation, you will be feeling particularly hemmed in today and it will be harder than usual to toe the line. Before you make any rash decisions or do something impulsive to let off steam, try to weigh up all the pros and cons.

• *Tuesday 4 April* •

You're not afraid to express some very deep feelings today and someone may be quite taken aback by the intensity of your emotions. They may even feel that you're being overly dramatic and will wonder why you're making such a song and dance about something that they consider to be relatively unimportant. If you want to be taken more seriously, you may have to spell things out to them.

• *Wednesday 5 April* •

This is an excellent day to promote yourself in a professional capacity. You can win people over and impress them with your knowledge and expertise. You have the confidence to present yourself with authority, which gives people faith in you and your abilities. Capitalize on your position of strength by suggesting any positive changes that you feel are necessary.

• *Thursday 6 April* •

You need to watch what you eat today because any over-indulgence with food or drink could cause a digestive upset, even if your stomach is usually quite robust. It's a good idea to review your diet in general, and if you feel you've put on weight recently perhaps it's time to cut out those extra treats for a while until you shed a few pounds. Finding a form of exercise that suits you will also get you in trim and improve your sense of well-being.

• *Friday 7 April* •

You will have to tread a fine line today between wanting your own way and taking somebody else's wishes into consideration. Rather than automatically assuming that you are viewing things from the right angle and everyone else is deluded, you may have to admit that other people's points of view are just as valid as yours. Only then will you be able to decide which is the best course of action to take.

• *Saturday 8 April* •

Today will be out of the ordinary in every way and you certainly won't be able to complain about being bored. A distant relative could suddenly make contact and shed light on a part of your family history that you knew nothing about. There are some unusual discoveries to be made and you could end up seeing yourself in a whole new way. You might also discover the answer to a mystery now.

• *Sunday 9 April* •

If you are a true Sagittarian, you know that it's never too late to change and you try to take as broad a point of view as possible. Today, in particular, you're more than willing to learn about yourself and alter a particular aspect of your behaviour. Is this because someone has dropped some hints or given you some constructive feedback, or are you simply aware that it's time to move on?

• *Monday 10 April* •

You can develop some important skills today if you're able to be patient and view your life in the long term. Be willing to learn from others and have the humility to recognize your mistakes if you go wrong. You can pave the way to living life more on your terms and you will reap great rewards if you are prepared to learn from experience and try to understand your true self.

• *Tuesday 11 April* •

Take care today because you could be facing a moral dilemma that pulls you in two different directions. You'll need to examine your position very carefully and try to decide where you honestly feel your loyalties lie. Once you've done that, the right choice will be obvious and you will know what to do next. What a relief that will be!

• *Wednesday 12 April* •

You are wearing your heart on your sleeve today, and this is likely to boost your popularity more than anything else. People will appreciate your openness and they will especially like the way you can sympathize with how they are feeling. So don't be surprised if a loved one confides in you because they know you will understand.

• *Thursday 13 April* •

Your romantic imagination is stimulated today and you're in the mood to be swept off your feet. There's no point in trying to take an objective view of any potential love interest because at the moment you are feeling very idealistic, so you will probably gloss over any flaws or imperfections in you-know-who. You might as well enjoy being in a rosy bubble today – provided you don't make any major decisions that call for a cool head!

• *Friday 14 April* •

If you feel the deck is stacked against you today, your best bet is to wait until tomorrow's planetary reshuffle. However frustrated you feel right now, especially because of delays or misunderstandings, bear in mind that this situation is only temporary. You might as well reconcile yourself to a day of minor hiccups, and do the best you can with the resources you've got.

• *Saturday 15 April* •

Your Sagittarian spontaneity comes to the fore today and you'll express your emotions exactly as you feel them, without holding anything back. Not only that, you'll also stand up for yourself if you feel that someone is getting at you. This can be very positive if someone has been keeping you in the dark recently because the truth can now come to light.

• *Sunday 16 April* •

If you have been at daggers drawn with a certain person recently, this is a wonderful day to call a truce. An intimate alliance that's been through a stormy patch can now be healed, as you become more aware of how much you value your relationship. One of you may have been disappointed by the other in some way, but you can now see that your expectations were far too high. It's time to be realistic.

• *Monday 17 April* •

Talk about places to go and people to see! You're caught up in the social whirl today and having a wonderful time. If you happen to find like-minded souls at whatever function or party you attend, this will make it an even more enjoyable occasion. So let your hair down, and make the most of the fact that life has a lot to offer you today.

• *Tuesday 18 April* •

You're not averse to using your charm to wind someone round your finger today, but unless you truly like this person they will quickly recognize that you're not being sincere. As long as you are genuine in your feelings, you will more than likely get what you want now. But be willing to compromise, just in case that winning smile doesn't work.

• *Wednesday 19 April* •

You're in danger of going off half-cocked today and acting rashly without thinking. The problem is that the more someone tries to get you to slow down and take stock of what you're doing, the more restless and headstrong you will become. Try to rein yourself in and see how you can best use your excess energy without getting yourself into hot water.

• *Thursday 20 April* •

Your mind is able to plumb the depths today and come up with some answers that have been eluding you until now.

Think of it as fitting the last jigsaw piece into the puzzle and finally being able to see the whole picture. What you do with this new perspective is up to you, but at the very least it should enable you to get ahead and see things more clearly.

• *Friday 21 April* •

This is a good day to finalize any agreements or commit to something that means a lot to you. You will do your best to fulfil whatever you take on today, and you have every intention of keeping your word. Try to set aside some time today to relax and take life easy. You won't want to rush around like a scalded cat – instead, you will prefer to put your feet up and let someone else do all the running!

• *Saturday 22 April* •

Find a good outlet for your abundant physical energy today, otherwise you will wind up feeling frustrated and spoiling for a fight. If you have a strong competitive streak, this would be an ideal day to take part in a competition, either as an individual or as part of a team. Not only will you enjoy this immensely, you might also get the added satisfaction of winning!

• *Sunday 23 April* •

Although you're still raring to go, you're much more likely to channel your energies into socializing today. You are far more interested in being with unusual people who give you food for thought rather than conventional types. If you are going to any form of social gathering you will certainly provide plenty of stimulus – you'll make sure of that! Don't be surprised if you turn someone's head or have an unexpected encounter.

• *Monday 24 April* •

Don't rely on first impressions unless you're absolutely sure they're reliable today. This is one occasion when giving someone the benefit of the doubt could seriously backfire on you. Ask lots of questions to ascertain exactly who you're dealing with, and if you have any reservations about this person, give them a wide berth. Forewarned is forearmed.

• *Tuesday 25 April* •

You will need to draw on your diplomatic skills today in order to tell someone a home truth they may not be ready to face up to. However much you sweeten the pill, there's no easy way to handle this situation. On the plus side, if they have confidence in you and your opinions, you can at least offer them some helpful advice that might help.

• *Wednesday 26 April* •

Don't know if you're coming or going? If you're fraught with tension today it's probably because one part of you is trying to toe the line while another part of you is trying to break free. You need to find a balance between having a structure to your life while still feeling that you can change things if they're no longer working.

• *Thursday 27 April* •

If you still feel stressed today, why not treat yourself to a massage or some other kind of relaxing treatment? Your shoulders are probably hunched up around your ears through tension, and it will do your body and mind the power of good to unwind and let go. A lovely warm bath with something sweet-smelling in it would be a wonderful way to wash your cares away.

• *Friday 28 April* •

Avoid the temptation to put yourself down or allow anyone else to undermine you today. Your self-esteem may not be at an all-time high but that doesn't mean that you should be negative about yourself. Relax by doing something really enjoyable, especially if it is sociable or allows you to mix with some of your favourite people. Curling up with a good book or a favourite TV programme will also be enjoyable.

• *Saturday 29 April* •

You feel at peace with the world today. You've got all the support you need from your nearest and dearest and you're heartened to know that they still believe in you. Give a special relationship the attention it deserves this weekend and try to stop other things from intruding on your time together. However, you may have to minister to someone who isn't feeling very well.

• *Sunday 30 April* •

The next two weeks are the perfect opportunity to think about your current working situation. Are you happy with the way things are going or do you know that there is room for improvement? While you're about it, have a think about the state of your health at the moment. It's a good time to seek some expert advice if you're worried about an ailment or symptom.

MAY AT A GLANCE

Love	♥ ♥ ♥
Money	£ $
Career	💻 💻 💻 💻 💻
Health	☼ ☼ ☼ ☼ ☼

• *Monday 1 May* •

If you're wondering where everyone is when you need them, it might be worthwhile thinking about why some people in your life don't seem to be all that reliable. It could be that part of you doesn't want to be obligated or tied down, and so you attract friends of a similar disposition. This is all fine and dandy when you're having fun, but disappointing when you're looking for support.

• *Tuesday 2 May* •

Sagittarians have a strong belief that we should all feel free to be our true selves. Unless you are an exception to this rule, you will want to do just that today. You're simply not interested in playing a stereotypical role or conforming to other people's expectations of you at the moment, and if you're not accepted on your terms you are willing to cut your losses and look elsewhere.

• *Wednesday 3 May* •

There is the distinct possibility of misunderstandings and muddles today. But before you get on your high horse and start complaining when things go wrong, you must be very clear in your own mind about where you stand or you will also find it difficult to make yourself understood. There's some confusion surrounding how you really feel about something, and you might be wise to allow the fog to dispel before you say anything.

• *Thursday 4 May* •

A conversation with someone you have great respect for could have a very sobering effect on you now and give you plenty of food for thought. Once you're in a serious frame of mind, you may well decide to review the way you're approaching your everyday life. Although you'd hate to think that you're stuck in an old pattern or rut, even you can hold on for too long. Perhaps it's time to cut free in some way?

• *Friday 5 May* •

You can work long and hard today without even breaking into a sweat! Whatever it is that you're involved in will completely absorb you and the time will fly by without you even noticing. If you're working on something that requires intuitive thinking and quick decisions, there'll be no doubt in your mind about what you need to do.

• *Saturday 6 May* •

It's not a day for keeping yourself to yourself because you could meet someone that you feel strongly attracted to. In some ways this person will seem mysterious and enigmatic and, although this is definitely part of their fascination, you'd be wise to ask yourself if they have something to hide. Find out more about them before you completely succumb to their charms. Better to be safe than sorry!

• *Sunday 7 May* •

'Make hay while the sun shines' sums up your philosophy today. You're either feeling very extravagant or extremely carefree – or both! Any recommendation not to overdo it would probably go in one ear and out the other. The fact is, you're feeling very confident about yourself and see no earthly reason why you shouldn't squeeze every moment of enjoyment you can out of life.

• *Monday 8 May* •

Don't be surprised if someone close needs a shoulder to cry on today. And yes, they are heading straight for yours! You won't have any problems offering your support and you'll even be glad that this person felt able to confide in you. Somehow you know exactly what to say to comfort and reassure them, and simply knowing how much you care will give them the boost they need.

• *Tuesday 9 May* •

If you've got exams coming up, this is a great day to hit your revision hard because you'll absorb much more than usual. There's no need to miss out if you aren't doing any studying because you will have increased powers of concentration. Make a point of doing something that will take advantage of your added brainpower, especially if you find that your attention normally tends to wander.

• *Wednesday 10 May* •

Check which way you're going today because you could be heading in the wrong direction. It really depends on what's in the driving seat – your head or your heart. If you're making a rational decision about a personal matter but you're still not sure if you're doing the right thing, allow your feelings to tell you where your real needs lie. You also need to keep your head screwed on the right way at work.

• *Thursday 11 May* •

It's a day for looking long and hard at the framework of your everyday life. Does it support you in the way you would like or do you feel as though you are floundering in a vacuum? Sagittarians need a purpose to their lives and this may be what you feel you're lacking. Think about what or who would add more substance and greater meaning to your everyday life. How can you make this happen?

• *Friday 12 May* •

You're in the mood to entertain and you may even feel like throwing a party today. What matters is that you're among friends and enjoying their company, so try not to spend too much time alone. If you can't do any entertaining at home, how about going out on the town? If your budget can stretch to it – or even if it can't – you'll probably feel like having a rip-roaring time. The last thing you want is to stint yourself!

• *Saturday 13 May* •

Do you feel as though you're backed into a corner with no escape route? If so, it's probably because of problems connected with commitments. Perhaps you are feeling reluctant to be pinned down or you are worried that someone is expecting too much from you. You may be tempted to hedge your bets but if this hasn't worked in the past it is unlikely to do much good now. Instead, you need to adopt a fresh approach.

• *Sunday 14 May* •

You will be in such a benevolent mood over the next two weeks that you will want to give freely of yourself and be generous with everything you have. Other people's welfare will be more important than your own, and you'll do whatever you can to give a hand to those who need your support. Some people are going to feel that all their Christmases have come at once! It will also be a marvellous time to take part in a discussion or negotiation.

• *Monday 15 May* •

If you feel as though you have become a slave to routine recently, you'll soon stir up some action today. If you feel like trying something new, why not experiment with a few ideas and see what you come up with. Perhaps you need to take off and discover a whole new world that will open you up to new dimensions in yourself. It might not be as far away as you think.

• *Tuesday 16 May* •

Even though you're absolutely determined to get your own way today, you've already decided that you're not going to ruffle any feathers in the process if you can possibly help it. Whatever your approach, you know that a certain amount of diplomacy, and maybe even a little flattery, will do more for your cause than any strong-arm tactics.

• *Wednesday 17 May* •

You've got so much nervous energy today that you won't know when to stop. On the plus side, you can cover a lot of ground and do things in half the time it would normally take you. The down side is that you may end up dropping with exhaustion so you put yourself out of action for a while. If you give yourself short breaks throughout the day you won't burn yourself out.

• *Thursday 18 May* •

Listen carefully to what a friend has to say today. They could offer you a new perspective on something that's been bothering you, and you might even realize that you've been making a big fuss about nothing. If someone else is involved, it's now up to you to defuse the situation – even if that means eating humble pie. This may not be your favourite way of kissing and making up, but if that's what it takes, so be it.

• *Friday 19 May* •

You will strongly defend a personal belief with anyone who challenges your opinion today, but go carefully, otherwise you could take it all too seriously and end up feeling as though you're the one under attack, rather than what you believe. Taking a criticism too personally will only trigger your anger and make you react in self-defence. If that happens, you could lose both respect and credibility.

• *Saturday 20 May* •

You may still be feeling oversensitive about what happened yesterday. You will either feel like hiding away to lick your wounds, or you'll be coming out from your corner ready to do battle. Maybe a totally different approach would heal the rift? Perhaps you should do some soul-searching, and ask yourself whether you share the responsibility for the whole argument with the other person. Was it six of one and half a dozen of the other?

• *Sunday 21 May* •

You need to curb your impatience and make an extra effort to be tolerant today, even though you may not feel like it. Your mind is working at the speed of light, and there will be times when you'll feel exasperated by the slow progress that certain people are making. You will long to chivvy them along but it might be better to let them proceed at their own pace unless you are working to an impossible deadline.

• *Monday 22 May* •

You're not exactly going at a snail's pace, but you have slowed down from yesterday's surge of energy – much to the relief of everyone around you! Although it's important to you that you keep your life moving forward, you recognize the value of taking stock and even standing still sometimes. If you do exactly that today, you'll generate the energy and focus you need in order to take the next step.

• *Tuesday 23 May* •

You want to be surrounded by friends and family today because you are in need of feeling that you belong to them. You particularly want to spend time with the people you share a long history with because you feel so at home with them and you can be your true self. The knowledge that you are accepted for who you are, warts and all, will make you feel uplifted and may even help to heal some emotional wounds.

• *Wednesday 24 May* •

What's that rattling sound? It could be a couple of skeletons that tumble out of a closet today – or perhaps you will willingly expose them to the light. If you are honest with yourself, you will realize that you need to face up to certain aspects of your character. You may not be very keen on them, and you may not even be very proud of them, but it's time to acknowledge them instead of pretending they don't exist. Only then can you do something about them.

• *Thursday 25 May* •

You can count on a strong show of affection and support over the next month. This will give you exactly the confirmation you need concerning the path you're on, and those who are willing to tread it with you. This may mean that you have to let go of one or two people who will no longer play a part in your life. If you accept this fact with good grace and appreciate everyone who is still around, you will find that life goes with a swing.

• *Friday 26 May* •

In spite of the recent ups and downs, you can now see your way ahead. You're aware of which areas of your life need improvement and, although you know this isn't an overnight process and Rome wasn't built in a day, you can at least set the ball rolling. However, watch out for someone who seems to be breathing fire or who wants to drag up some past history and make a big fuss. It's not you, is it?

• *Saturday 27 May* •

If you simply allow the day to unfold without making any particular plans, you'll create a lot more room for spontaneity and, as a result, you will really enjoy yourself. Yes, it's one of those delicious days when you are happy to take life as it comes. Somebody may even surprise you by giving you a treat or you might receive an unexpected invitation. Go with the flow and you won't be disappointed.

• *Sunday 28 May* •

You're strongly influenced by your emotions today, and any decisions you make will be based more on how you feel than what you think. Fortunately, you should be feeling very positive and will be able to trust your gut feelings to make the right choice. You've got a good understanding of the current situation and you want to make the best of it. Good luck!

• *Monday 29 May* •

Having some wonderfully creative ideas isn't enough for you today. You want to convert them into something real and put them into action. There's no more sitting on the sidelines contemplating your navel – you want to see if dreams really do come true. Decide what you would like to happen in your life and, if you feel it's within your reach, go for it. Yet, even if it seems like an impossible dream, it could still come true.

• *Tuesday 30 May* •

If it's mental stimulation you're looking for today, you've got it in spades. Friends and colleagues are only too happy for you to bounce your ideas off them, and the feedback they give you could inspire you to greater heights. This could be the day that you discover you have a talent for writing or some other creative activity. So don't be bashful or falsely modest. Enjoy putting your talents to the test!

• *Wednesday 31 May* •

The domino effect seems to be in operation today, because it appears that whatever changes you make in your own life have a knock-on effect on the lives of those close to you. This can be extraordinarily positive and rewarding, provided you're aware of the impression you make and you are willing to take responsibility for the influence you have. Unfortunately, other people may not be so aware of the impression they are making, and as a result you may want to give them a wide berth.

JUNE AT A GLANCE

Love	♥ ♥ ♥ ♥ ♥
Money	£ $
Career	💻 💻 💻
Health	☼ ☼ ☼

• *Thursday 1 June* •

There could be fireworks on the relationship front today unless one of you is willing to back down. Just because you think you can win doesn't justify going into battle and, in any case, it would be a far greater victory to do something that strengthens your partnership. You will be better off if you offer an olive branch and save your fighting spirit for a more appropriate occasion.

• *Friday 2 June* •

You should be feeling more at ease with yourself today and this will reflect in everything around you. For a start, yesterday's contentious mood has given way to a much more conciliatory feeling. Peace and harmony are what you're looking for, and you'll make whatever adjustments are necessary to achieve this. It should all come quite naturally, you'll be pleased to know. What's more, this urge for harmony will be at the back of your mind during the next two weeks.

• *Saturday 3 June* •

There are powerful planetary energies at work in your love life today and you'll be feeling anything but lukewarm. Either the passion has reignited between you and your partner, or you've just met someone and feel as though you've been hit by a ten-ton lorry. You are definitely smitten, and it looks as though the temperature is set to soar this weekend, whatever the weather!

• *Sunday 4 June* •

There's a hint of magic in the air today and everything flows without any effort on your part. Magnificent! It's one of those days when all seems well with the world and you're feeling glad to be alive. Although you know this intoxicated state can't last forever, at least for today you can enjoy the luxury of being completely carefree. Make the most of it!

• *Monday 5 June* •

Are you ready to be in the spotlight? Put as much positive energy as you can into your work and you'll reap all sorts of unexpected benefits today. If you've been trying to get someone influential to notice you, whatever you do today to make your mark stands a good chance of coming to their attention. Your star is in the ascendant and it's your time to shine.

• *Tuesday 6 June* •

You're about to experience a whole range of new emotional situations that will be very different from anything you have felt before. Someone makes a big impact on you and consequently acts as a catalyst for you, putting you in touch with some deep and intense feelings that you never knew you had. If you see this as a journey into yourself, it promises to be one you'll never forget.

• *Wednesday 7 June* •

Whoever first said 'everything in moderation' wasn't thinking of Sagittarians! You're in one of those self-indulgent moods again where you don't want to put any limits on yourself. This means that you'll be tempted to overspend, overeat and anything else you can think of that's fun. Self-control is not in your vocabulary today so you might as well live now and (here's the rub) pay later.

• *Thursday 8 June* •

This is a good day to take a dispassionate look at your lifestyle and see if there are any habits you've acquired that aren't doing you any favours. If you decide that there are and you've got the willpower to change, find the best way to go about it. Although old patterns are often hard to break, you're more resolute than usual at the moment and so you can move mountains if you set your mind to it.

• *Friday 9 June* •

Friendships of all kinds are highlighted today and you can thank your lucky stars that you have more than your fair share of them. You may well feel in need of a heart-to-heart and, if so, there'll be no shortage of people who are there for you. It doesn't matter how you're feeling, you simply know that the support will be unconditional.

• *Saturday 10 June* •

You might not accomplish very much today in practical terms, but you'll be doing a lot of planning in your head which will feel just as productive. Whether you're thinking about a holiday or mulling over a new idea that you want to try out, you've got plenty to occupy your mind. Don't forget to get some exercise at some stage in the day – it's not only your brain that needs a work-out!

• *Sunday 11 June* •

Yesterday's brainstorming session has more than likely given you a new and totally original perspective on both your personal and professional lives. The changes that you want to make now could range from radically rethinking the direction you're heading in to altering your appearance in some way. You will probably opt for something in between the two, but don't be scared of going for broke if you know it's necessary.

• *Monday 12 June* •

Fortune smiles on you today and any creative endeavour will go well, especially if it is connected with your career. A lucky break could come out of the blue and give you the chance to show off your talents to their full potential. An influential admirer may spot you and they could even make you an offer you'll find hard to refuse. Wait until your feet touch the ground before you accept.

• *Tuesday 13 June* •

To say that you're feeling amorous today would be an understatement! All you want to do is shower your loved one with affection, and if you can't do it in person you'll find some other way of letting them know how much you care. If you're not in a relationship, this is definitely not a day to be on your own or you'll feel really lonely. Go out and socialize.

• *Wednesday 14 June* •

Congratulations! You can rest on your laurels today and feel justifiably good about yourself. Although you know you still have a long way to go, you're able to acknowledge how far you've come. You've struck a good balance between being flexible and open and yet keeping some kind of structure and continuity to your everyday life. No wonder you're smiling!

• *Thursday 15 June* •

You could be involved in an intense and heated discussion today with someone who challenges you to think on your feet. This may or may not be threatening, depending on what's at stake. If it feels important that you stand your ground and try to gain the upper hand, make sure you do it for the right reasons and not simply to score points.

• *Friday 16 June* •

People are more than willing to support you over the coming fortnight. However, you will need to be very aware of yourself and how you interact with others in order to avoid being at cross-purposes with them. Provided you honestly evaluate your intentions and know what you are doing, you won't face the difficulties that you encountered in yesterday's contretemps. Quite the opposite, in fact.

• *Saturday 17 June* •

The last couple of days may have tested your patience but they have also helped to make you more tolerant. You certainly feel more magnanimous in your attitude and you might even have gained a little humility. This is an ideal opportunity to break free from any old negativity and see your world in much broader and more expansive terms.

• *Sunday 18 June* •

Set aside some time today to enjoy your own company and do things at your own pace. A whole day of contemplation would be a wonderful way to give yourself space, doing whatever most inspires you. There may be some emotions bubbling away beneath the surface that you need to get in touch with. It shouldn't take you long to discover what they are and what to do with them.

• *Monday 19 June* •

You may get the chance to boost your earnings today or make some kind of long-term investment to ensure greater financial security. You're keen to put your income on a stronger footing and you're ready to spot the opportunities that will help you do that. Your confidence about your job prospects is looking good and whatever you do now is bound to pay dividends.

• *Tuesday 20 June* •

You're very emotionally attuned to your partner's needs today and you have a strong desire to spend time together. Both of you want to make the relationship a priority and you'll be tempted to put the rest of the world on hold while you focus on each other. If you can do this without anyone else kicking up a fuss, by all means follow your heart. Otherwise, you may have to compromise.

• *Wednesday 21 June* •

You won't be able to suffer fools gladly today and, if you don't curb your impulses for the next 24 hours, you may end up saying something you will regret. The problem with being direct and calling a spade a spade in this instance is that it will probably fall on deaf ears, adding to your frustration. Be aware that you're operating on a short fuse and take counter measures.

• *Thursday 22 June* •

You're in an ideal position to make sense of what's happening around you and to put right any misunderstandings that may have occurred recently. You probably couldn't see the wood for the trees before but you now have a clearer picture – much to your relief. You're more than willing to learn from the past if it will help you to plan for the future.

• *Friday 23 June* •

It's all hands on deck today and the strong sense of cooperation between you and others means that the more you can pull together for a common goal, the more you'll accomplish. Your joint purpose is more important than any personal considerations that any of you may have, and if there are any differences between you you're determined not to let them rock the boat.

• *Saturday 24 June* •

Whatever the weather is today, the home fires are burning brightly for you. All you want to do is to put your feet up and enjoy the pleasures of your home comforts. You will be able to appreciate many simple things that you were in danger of taking for granted. You may even view a family member with fresh eyes, as it dawns on you how little you really know them.

• *Sunday 25 June* •

Go carefully today because there is a good chance that you could lose your rag with someone or finally become so exasperated with them that you say something awful in the heat of the moment. This will help you to get certain things off your chest but it could sour the atmosphere or cause some bad feeling between you. Try to minimize the damage by making your point and then changing the subject.

• *Monday 26 June* •

Although you would prefer to mind your own business and not become embroiled in other people's disagreements, someone seems intent on getting you to mediate and they won't take no for an answer. Your Sagittarian fair-mindedness is just what's needed to defuse the situation. However, you may be amused when you realize how easy it is to sort out other people's problems and how tricky it can be to resolve your own dilemmas. Oh well, that's life!

• *Tuesday 27 June* •

Your self-confidence is put to the test today but it looks as though you'll sail through with flying colours. Whatever anyone throws at you is unlikely even to ruffle your feathers because you are feeling so cool, calm and collected. In fact, you'll probably secretly relish someone trying to put you off your stroke because you know full well that they have no chance of succeeding.

• *Wednesday 28 June* •

There are gremlins about today and everything you plan for seems to get sabotaged in some way. You might as well hold fire until you feel that this disruptive element is no longer operating, because to go ahead under these conditions would only cause chaos. Be especially careful when doing anything connected with your work or health, because all sorts of things could go haywire.

• *Thursday 29 June* •

Talk about chomping at the bit! You've got so much energy and so many ideas today that the thought of having to hold back and bide your time while other people get their act together is almost unbearable. Without losing your momentum, it might be a good idea to find an enjoyable distraction to take your mind off the boredom of being in limbo.

• *Friday 30 June* •

Somebody will take you under their wing over the next few months and give you a few invaluable tips. Whether this person is a teacher, mentor or boss, they will gain your respect and admiration. The lessons you learn from them will stand you in good stead for a long time to come. What's more, you can expect a lot of laughter along the way because this person will be terrific company.

JULY AT A GLANCE

Love	♥ ♥ ♥ ♥ ♥
Money	£ $ £ $ £
Career	💻 💻
Health	☼

• *Saturday 1 July* •

You start the month on a high note and you're determined to get a lot done this July. In fact, you're so fired up that you may even exceed your own expectations of what you feel able to achieve. Setting yourself goals for the month ahead will have a very positive effect on you and give you a strong sense of purpose. You've got the green light, so all you need to do now is to move into top gear.

• *Sunday 2 July* •

So much is falling into place and you're beginning to see the pattern of your life with much more clarity than before. You don't want to leave any stone unturned, and if you feel there are still important issues to discuss with a partner or loved one, now's the time to do it. You will be able to talk about sensitive or potentially embarrassing issues with no trouble at all, yet you will still consider the other person's feelings. Terrific!

• *Monday 3 July* •

Your thoughts turn to journeys and travel today, or anything else that will let you expand your current horizons. The entire prospect of travelling may be so seductive and enticing that you're already halfway there in your imagination! If you decide to go ahead, double check all the travel arrangements when you book to avoid any potential hiccups.

• *Tuesday 4 July* •

You're in two minds about something today and the harder you try to make a decision, the more confused you will become. You may feel as though you're going round in circles. You really need to detach yourself emotionally from the situation and put some space between you and the dilemma. Only then can you reach a conclusion based on what you want, as opposed to what is expected of you.

• *Wednesday 5 July* •

It's full steam ahead today because yesterday's uncertainties have given way to a much more assertive you. You can now decide on which course of action you want to take without feeling compromised by other people's needs or expectations. You've got the bit between your teeth, and to say you're feeling headstrong would be understating it. You're ready and willing, so go for it!

• *Thursday 6 July* •

You could be called upon to lend a sympathetic ear to a close friend or colleague who's in need of a heart-to-heart today. Although you're more than happy to help, you may discover that they require a lot more than you're able to give. Rather than feel you have to come up with all the answers, admit your limitations and see what you can realistically do.

• *Friday 7 July* •

If you feel you've been languishing on a back burner in your career recently and wondering when you'll have a change of fortune, you could be in for a very pleasant surprise today. You'll just happen to be in the right place at the right time and everything else will follow naturally. It may boost your confidence still further to dress up if you're going somewhere important or official.

• *Saturday 8 July* •

Strictly speaking, it may not be the right time for a spring clean, but this is still an excellent day to blow away the cobwebs and have a good clear-out at home. Enlist the support of as many family members as possible because you'll be amazed by how much gets done. The only problem you might come up against is if there are too many chiefs and not enough Indians. Take charge!

• *Sunday 9 July* •

Depending on how well things went yesterday, this could be a day of either domestic bliss or hidden tensions! If you've worked in harmony with other people and you're satisfied with what you accomplished, the chances are that you're feeling very close and affectionate with the people around you. If you somehow didn't quite pull together as you had hoped, there may be a mess to clear up – in more ways than one!

• *Monday 10 July* •

You're so finely tuned today that you can pick up everyone's emotions without even trying. This can be a blessing as well as a curse because, although other people will appreciate you being so aware of how they're feeling, you won't particularly want to pick up on any negative emotions that they are sending out. Make sure you don't lose track of your own feelings.

• *Tuesday 11 July* •

The truth about one particular relationship comes to light today and it's better that you face the reality of the situation rather than continue to turn a blind eye. One of you hasn't been living up to the demands and obligations of the agreements you made, and it's time you reviewed the state of play between you. What you both need to decide is where to go from here.

• *Wednesday 12 July* •

You can't afford to take anything at face value today and you'll need to read between the lines if you want to avoid misunderstanding what is going on. If someone isn't being completely honest with you, the first thing you need to ascertain is whether this is deliberate or unintentional. You'll need a lot of guile and diplomacy to get to the bottom of this one, so go carefully.

• *Thursday 13 July* •

Nothing and no one can hold you back from doing what you want to do over the next three weeks. You're in no mood to compromise and, because you mean business, you'll more than likely accomplish whatever it is you set out to do. It's not often that you feel so free to pursue your goals, so when you do manage to create an opportunity it's no wonder that you're unstoppable!

• *Friday 14 July* •

You're convinced you've got the Midas touch today and that your optimism alone will turn everything to gold. It's true that a positive attitude can transform many situations, but you may be overestimating what is actually feasible. Even so, you will make things happen if you can combine planning and foresight with your unique ability to spot an opportunity.

• *Saturday 15 July* •

You're the beneficiary of someone's generosity today and you may wonder what you did to deserve such lavish attention.

Not that you'll want to shun such a showering of abundance or give yourself a bad time about being unworthy! Instinctively, you know that what goes around comes around and that one day you give, and on another you receive.

• *Sunday 16 July* •

You probably feel like a quiet day at home today to give yourself time to prepare for the week ahead. Recharging and building up energy is important over the next fortnight if you want to stay in good shape and not succumb to the symptoms of stress and other maladies. Your body needs to be pampered occasionally, so give it the five-star treatment and see how wonderful it can feel.

• *Monday 17 July* •

If you ever thought you could write a book, or even a short story, let your imagination run wild today and you might discover you have a talent after all. Tapping into your innate creativity in whichever way most appeals will be a source of immense joy and inspiration, and even if it doesn't lead to great things the pleasure and enjoyment alone will make it worthwhile.

• *Tuesday 18 July* •

Do you wish you could get away from it all today? You always enjoy anything that expands your mind and gives you something new to think about, and you're certainly provided with lots of food for thought today. Any kind of travel or cultural activity will stimulate your thirst for new experiences and indulge your need for some escapism. The big, wide world is beckoning!

• *Wednesday 19 July* •

At best, you're feeling rather pensive and nostalgic today but you might equally be feeling somewhat melancholy. Is that because you're missing someone whom you haven't seen in ages? If you feel like getting back in touch but you're not sure how they'll respond, give yourself a little time to get used to the idea before making the first move.

• *Thursday 20 July* •

You're able to compartmentalize things mentally today and this tactic will enable you to work with extra efficiency. You're undaunted by the workload that's piling up because you're confident that you've got the resources and the stamina to get through it all. You will probably prefer to get on alone, rather than risk having a spanner thrown in the works by someone who doesn't know your system.

• *Friday 21 July* •

You're very good at communicating with others today and as a result you're keen for everyone to say what's on their mind. You may even call a family meeting so that everyone gets a chance to speak up. And it's not just at home that you're promoting freedom of expression. You'll happily encourage everyone around you to open up and say what they think.

• *Saturday 22 July* •

Give yourself a pat on the back today for everything that you've been able to achieve so far. Although you've probably got a list as long as your arm of goals yet to realize, you can still tick off a few things that you set your heart on and managed to accomplish. Over the coming four weeks you will get the chance to aim for even greater success, and you could also receive some fabulous opportunities. There will be everything to play for!

• *Sunday 23 July* •

There's a strong emotional quality to everything you do today and you will feel happiest with close family and friends. Even if all you do is relax and enjoy their company, it will feel like a day well spent. A very special connection with one particular friend or relative will deepen in some way as you get to know each other better. You will enjoy a rosy glow of contentment as a result.

• *Monday 24 July* •

Make sure you do everything by the book today because if you take any shortcuts or break the rules you'll end up with egg on your face. You'll probably have to curb your impatience more than once but if you're methodical in your approach, you'll be much more productive than if you attack things like a bull in a china shop. If you suspect that you're operating on a short fuse, tell everyone to stand well back.

• *Tuesday 25 July* •

Are you ready to take a chance? You're certainly contemplating taking a gamble on something, but you've already weighed up the odds and you feel sure that you've got nothing to lose. Taking a calculated risk will add some spice to your life and provide you with the challenge you need. Whatever the outcome is, you know that being true to yourself always pays off.

• *Wednesday 26 July* •

You're able to inspire trust in other people today, especially if they can help you to get on in life. You will know instinctively what is the right thing to say to them, especially if you need to patch up a recent quarrel or you want to get to know them better. Because you're so effective at getting the best out of people, they in turn will want to help you in any way they can.

Such a mutually beneficial exchange will set the stage for greater things.

• *Thursday 27 July* •

You believe you can overcome virtually any obstacle that may crop up today. It's a fabulous feeling! Your timing is immaculate and you know exactly when to act and when to hold back, which gives you the advantage in your dealings with others. Don't underestimate your ability to read a situation and respond accordingly – it's something you can draw on more than you realize.

• *Friday 28 July* •

Life is looking pretty good today. Things may go your way or you may simply feel that everything will work out for the best in the long run. This is the sort of optimistic attitude that sets you apart from other members of the zodiac, and as a result you could bring a lot of comfort to someone who is finding life hard going at the moment. It might also mean that opportunities come your way because you have attracted them.

• *Saturday 29 July* •

Don't be surprised if you are attracted to someone today who isn't your usual cup of tea. They may come from a different walk of life or you might not look at them twice at any other time. You're not sure whether this is a sexual attraction or if it's purely platonic, but either way you feel compelled to get to know this person better. Whatever the connection is, they have something invaluable to teach you about yourself.

• *Sunday 30 July* •

Sagittarians often feel as if they have a guardian angel watching over them because help can arrive in the most unlikely guises and often at the eleventh hour. Today is no exception, and someone who has your best interests at heart is ready to give you a lot of support, especially if it's connected with finances or your job. You are not one to look a gift horse in the mouth, so you'll be more than happy for this person to give you a hand.

• *Monday 31 July* •

You can make quite an impression over the coming fortnight, so don't hide your light under a bushel. You will know how to handle people and what to say to them. What's more, you will be able to manipulate a situation to your advantage without being underhand or devious. This is especially likely if you've done your homework in advance. Provided you don't overstep the mark, you can't put a foot wrong now.

AUGUST AT A GLANCE

Love	♥ ♥ ♥
Money	£ $ £
Career	💻 💻 💻 💻 💻
Health	☼

• *Tuesday 1 August* •

It doesn't take a sledgehammer to crack a nut so be careful that you don't go to extremes over the next six weeks in an effort to change something you're not happy about. Coming on too strong will only force a stalemate or cause a lot of bad feeling. Everyone will be much more amenable to the idea of doing things differently if you can present a calm and reasonable front.

• *Wednesday 2 August* •

You may not be able to move mountains today but you can still make a lot happen. A project that you've put a lot of planning and thought into needs an extra burst of energy to get it off the ground. Reality and practicalities may prevent you from giving this your undivided attention but, even so, you can still manage to get it all done within the limited time you have.

• *Thursday 3 August* •

If you feel that your life is moving in a totally new direction but you can't clearly see the signposts yet, simply trust that you will be shown which way to go when the time is right. There is a lot happening behind the scenes that you aren't fully aware of, so you need to cultivate a combination of faith and patience at the moment. Don't worry – you'll do it!

• *Friday 4 August* •

It might be difficult to determine what you're feeling and how much of other people's emotions you're picking up today. If you have a strong reaction to someone and this seems disproportionate to the situation, you could be getting your wires crossed. Until you know what is going on and whether you are reading the situation correctly, it might be a wise move to step out of the fray for a while.

• *Saturday 5 August* •

You're raring to go today and the more activities you have planned the better. You'll only get bored and irritable if you don't have an outlet for all that energy, so make the most of your increased dynamism and try to set the world on fire! You may end up doing most things on your own now because not many people will be able to keep pace with you.

• *Sunday 6 August* •

The things you learn about yourself today will have a positive effect on every area of your life, but especially on your close friendships and partnerships. You're able to look at yourself, warts and all, and see where you may need to make adjustments. Perhaps you should lower certain expectations that you have of yourself and others. This will give you and everyone else the chance to be more yourselves rather than struggle to live up to such unrealistically high standards.

• *Monday 7 August* •

You are curious about the world at the best of times but you long to learn even more than usual over the next two weeks. How about studying a subject that has always intrigued you but which has remained a closed book until now? Alternatively, you might fancy learning a new language or you could find yourself in situations that require you to think on your feet and adapt to a lot of changes. You certainly won't be bored!

• *Tuesday 8 August* •

If you believe that honesty is the best policy, you may feel as if you have no choice but say what's on your mind today, in spite of the fact that you know that your words will go down like a ton of bricks. You probably feel that being direct and forthright is the only way to get the message across and that a more subtle approach would go in one ear and out the other.

• *Wednesday 9 August* •

You're on the move today and you won't want to stay in the same place for long. You have so many errands to run that you'll have to be super-organized if you're going to get everything done in time. Not everyone will be moving at your fast pace so you may have to leave them behind. Even so, don't rush through anything that's complicated or important because it will be easy to make silly mistakes.

• *Thursday 10 August* •

You could see a marked change in certain relationships over the next few months. Someone could be a source of tremendous support to you, making you feel that you can rely on them no matter what. Alternatively, an alliance may go through a shaky period, so that you wonder whether your partnership will emerge unscathed. If you meet someone new now, they may be a lot more serious than your usual choice of companion.

• *Friday 11 August* •

Whatever your usual routine is, today is going to be quite different. You need to expect the unexpected, and even then you may still be surprised. This may be pleasant or challenging, depending on how flexible and open you are. Someone you're close to may reveal a totally different side of themselves, throwing you temporarily off balance. Be prepared!

• *Saturday 12 August* •

You may have a strange feeling of *déja vu* today, either with a person that you meet and think you recognize or a place you visit for the first time that seems familiar. You'll be fascinated and perplexed by this and determined to get to the bottom of this weird puzzle. You may not discover the whys and wherefores, but you'll enjoy trying to solve the mystery.

• *Sunday 13 August* •

The feelgood factor is everywhere today and whatever you do is likely to go well. Your buoyant optimism is working well and this colours your whole attitude, making it a joy to be with you. You'll attract people to you like magnets, and your conversation will have an uplifting effect on everyone. No wonder you'll be the soul of popularity this Sunday!

• *Monday 14 August* •

Think about whether you need to make some changes to your career or your direction in life. Alternatively, you may be facing changes that feel as if they're being forced on you by circumstances beyond your control. However, perhaps it really is time that you made some adjustments to this area of your life? You don't have to do it all at once but maybe you should begin to set the ball rolling.

• *Tuesday 15 August* •

You are now feeling much more positive about the goal posts being changed than you were yesterday, and you can see more clearly how effective the new status quo will be. In fact, now that you no longer feel threatened, you may start to feel optimistic and eager to work out some new objectives that are more in tune with the changing world around you.

• *Wednesday 16 August* •

You may need to hold your horses today and think before you speak too hastily. At best, you're able to accurately perceive a situation and reflect it back to those concerned. Equally, however, what you believe to be an intuitive insight may be coloured by what you want to see, rather than what is really happening, and this is where you could go badly wrong. You need to be sure that you know what's what before making any snap decisions.

• *Thursday 17 August* •

It's easy to stand up for yourself today and, if anything, you may need to tone yourself down slightly. Not only do you want to do your own thing and not have anyone even so much as offer some advice, you also want to prove that you're a force to be reckoned with. Depending on how you go about this, you'll either intimidate or impress. It's up to you.

• *Friday 18 August* •

Are you feeling let down or disappointed? If so, it's important that you come to terms with how much of your own behaviour is responsible for your current state of mind. It may appear as if someone's critical attitude towards you is the source of your despondency but, if you're really honest with yourself, perhaps this person has a point and you can learn from it.

• *Saturday 19 August* •

You need to tread very carefully today to avoid stepping on someone's toes. It seems that unless you're willing to placate a loved one and adopt a conciliatory manner with them, they will make it very difficult for you to do whatever is on today's agenda. They would be much more willing to support you if they thought you weren't taking things for granted.

• *Sunday 20 August* •

You are given the perfect opportunity today to discuss your future plans with your nearest and dearest and find out how they really feel about them. You may have assumed that everyone was perfectly happy with the way you've been going about things, and missed some of the hints to the contrary. At least you can now straighten things out.

• *Monday 21 August* •

The emotional atmosphere around you is much more harmonious today and you can count on a lot more support than you have received over the past few days. Feeling more secure in yourself creates a solid base of operations from which to live your life and inspires more confidence in you from other people. It's only when you get carried away that you sometimes lose touch with reality.

• *Tuesday 22 August* •

Something or someone that you've been afraid of in the past no longer holds any power over you and you are feeling a great sense of relief. Now that you've exorcized that particular demon, you can begin to structure your life in such a way that you recognize when a fear is beginning to take control. At least that way you're able to feel more in charge of your destiny.

• *Wednesday 23 August* •

Setting yourself high standards today will pay off because the better you do a job, and the more of yourself that you invest in it, the greater the recognition you'll receive. Being too self-critical is undermining and unproductive, but striving to improve your performance will bring out the best in you. Going for gold is well within your reach now!

• *Thursday 24 August* •

Any success that you have today will owe more to hard work than luck. Although you still need to sustain the efforts you're currently making to realize your goals, nevertheless you can take pride in how far you've come. In any event, if you're a typical Sagittarian, it's the experiences you have along the way that are often more important than the destination itself.

• *Friday 25 August* •

There may be the odd storm cloud hanging over you today, which makes you feel slightly apprehensive. You're not in the mood to compromise, and neither is anyone else. This makes coming to an agreement extremely difficult, and any kind of team effort is at best challenging and at worst not likely to work. You may have to go it alone if you want to avoid a blow-up.

• *Saturday 26 August* •

There isn't a cloud on the horizon today, thank goodness, and the accent is on squeezing as much enjoyment as you can from the day. Ideally, you should have something sociable on the agenda. You may also feel like treating yourself to something new to wear, especially if there's someone you want to impress. Why not take a friend on your shopping spree?

• *Sunday 27 August* •

You aren't afraid of being yourself today no matter what situation you find yourself in. You are easy to be with and people who haven't met you before will be impressed by your relaxed and confident manner. You're able to shrug off any negative thoughts that might fleetingly pop into your head because you know that they are only passing fancies and have no connection with reality.

• *Monday 28 August* •

Someone is burying their head in the sand and doing their best to pretend that there isn't a problem. Although this doesn't affect you directly, you may decide that you're the best person to tackle the situation. As long as you maintain your emotional detachment, you will be much more effective than certain people who are feeling exasperated by current events. Keep your cool!

• *Tuesday 29 August* •

A faithful friend offers you some pearls of wisdom today that turn out to be priceless. You may not fully appreciate the value of what you've been given, but the passing of time will prove the worth of those words. This isn't the first time that you've been given some valuable advice, and you should feel grateful to be surrounded by such loyal supporters.

• *Wednesday 30 August* •

Your greatest pleasure today comes from learning something new. You are able to acquire information very quickly and, provided you're interested and inspired by what you're being taught, you'll quickly get the hang of what you are doing. You may even decide to put in some extra hours so you can get further ahead than the original target you set yourself.

• *Thursday 31 August* •

A family member is feeling left out or neglected in some way and you're in a quandary about how to reassure them. It's going to take more than putting an arm around them to cheer them up because the hurt goes deeper than they're willing to let on. Try to get to the bottom of this now and help this person to open up before they completely disappear into their shell.

SEPTEMBER AT A GLANCE

Love	♥ ♥
Money	£ $
Career	🖥 🖥 🖥 🖥 🖥
Health	☼

• Friday 1 September •

You could be stopped dead in your tracks today by an unexpected turn of events. Although this will be frustrating on one level, there is a silver lining to this particular cloud if only you can be patient enough to discover what it is. Look at the situation from all angles and something will emerge to show you the way forward. Trust that this is a blessing in disguise.

• Saturday 2 September •

Mentally and verbally you're at your best today, and the more friends you can see and talk to the happier you'll be. You are able to express yourself in such a way that you can reach people and connect with them. You've no time for small talk – you either want meaningful conversations or nothing. If an old dispute is still unresolved, you can now clear it up.

• Sunday 3 September •

A close relationship feels very special today and you'll want to spend as much time with this person as possible. Any barriers that existed between you before seem to have melted away and you're on completely the same wavelength. You may well have your differences but you're able, at least for today, to accept each other unconditionally.

• *Monday 4 September* •

Adjusting to everyday reality today is quite dispiriting and leaves you feeling strangely isolated, even if you're surrounded by people. You will need to make an extra effort to get back into your normal routine because this is probably the last thing you want to do. The best antidote to your current mood is an activity in which you can completely absorb yourself.

• *Tuesday 5 September* •

You can't keep a good Sagittarian down, and you're beginning to feel more upbeat and cheerful today. It's almost as if you need to compensate for feeling gloomy by seeing things in a more positive and optimistic light. Be careful, however, that you don't go from one extreme to the other, otherwise you'll end up wearing yourself out. Find a happy medium.

• *Wednesday 6 September* •

Whatever your emotional state is today, you are not prepared to hold back or compromise about the way you're feeling. It's important to you that you express yourself with honesty and, even if you're a majority of one, you're prepared to stand up for what you believe in. No doubt you will create a few waves by being so resolute but, as you know, life isn't always plain sailing.

• *Thursday 7 September* •

Provided you don't get bogged down in little details, you can be extremely productive over the coming three weeks and break the back of a project or job that you've been working on. You will have a very practical and methodical approach and you might even surprise yourself by how organized you are. By the time the month is over, you should feel immensely satisfied by what you've been able to accomplish.

• *Friday 8 September* •

You know without a shadow of a doubt who you can count on today. Someone who was more of a casual acquaintance than a friend will surprise you by pledging their support. There is every chance that your relationship with this person will become a lot more serious, and now that they've proven to you where they stand, you are ready to give them the benefit of the doubt.

• *Saturday 9 September* •

Be careful what you wish for today because it might come true! Think carefully about what it is you really want from life and how realistic such an aspiration truly is. Anything that is way beyond your reach right now is unlikely to happen, but if you set some realistic goals they could soon turn into reality.

• *Sunday 10 September* •

You are so articulate and persuasive today that you can get just about anyone to do anything for you. This will work very well for you provided you don't try to manipulate people into doing things that they really don't want to do. As long as they can see the point of doing things your way, they will be willing to cross hell and high water for you.

• *Monday 11 September* •

It's one of those tricky days when you may feel as though you have to be continually on the defensive. The result could be a lot of bad feeling unless you can keep your cool and deal with the situation in a calm and collected manner. Losing your temper will only make matters worse, and then it will be harder to plead your case. However indignant you are, you can only clear up this misunderstanding by keeping a level head.

• *Tuesday 12 September* •

You need to be as loose and flexible as possible today so that you can float a few ideas and see where they lead. Try to eliminate as many stressful activities as you can from your day so that you're free to think creatively. Following logical trains of thought will only lead to dead ends, whereas more inspired pathways can open you up to exciting new possibilities.

• *Wednesday 13 September* •

Being true to your Sagittarian Sun sign means that you love making plans for the future, and the coming fortnight is the ideal time to do just that. There's no point in trying to keep your feet on the ground because once you allow your imagination to run riot, you can come up with some truly grandiose schemes. Not every fantastic adventure you envisage will come to fruition, but you'll enjoy planning them nevertheless.

• *Thursday 14 September* •

Are you fed up with the same old routine? You're in the mood to be entertained today, particularly if it's something out of the ordinary. Any kind of cultural activity that is unusual or different from what you normally do would fit the bill. It doesn't really matter if it's serious or light-hearted, as long as it provides you with a fresh way of looking at life.

• *Friday 15 September* •

You have an increased sense of duty or responsibility today which is making you take things very seriously. A close friend or partner needs your support and you may have to drop everything in order to accommodate them. Your commitment to this person is being put to the test, as well as the validity of your relationship. One way or another, you'll know where you stand.

• *Saturday 16 September* •

You are feeling wonderfully optimistic today and in the mood to rise to a challenge. In other words, it's one of those days when you feel like your true self, and ready for any eventuality that comes along. If possible, try to visit somewhere new now, especially if the whole trip feels like an adventure. It's also a great day for organizing a future journey or trip, especially if it's a holiday.

• *Sunday 17 September* •

Between now and early November you need to think carefully about your career and your long-term goals. Is everything going according to plan or do you need to take some emergency action to get things back on track? Don't be surprised if you feel unusually ambitious over the next few weeks, and are extra determined to achieve what you set out to do. This is your chance to make a mark on the world!

• *Monday 18 September* •

All kinds of irrational fears may be trying to take hold of you today, and until you can get to grips with these you will feel as though you're going round in circles. You are probably playing imaginary scenarios in your mind and some of these are making you break out in a cold sweat. Allow your inner doubts to come to the surface and see if they are really as serious as you thought.

• *Tuesday 19 September* •

You need some positive distractions today to take your mind off things. Reading an absorbing book or listening to inspirational music will help to clear your head and get you back in balance. If you fancy doing something sociable, you will want to spend time with people who are unusual or unconventional in some way. Anyone who's a stick-in-the-mud will leave you colder than yesterday's bathwater.

• *Wednesday 20 September* •

Get set for a roller-coaster of a day, with hardly time to come up for air. Everything will move at a terrific pace, which you'll mostly find exhilarating and only occasionally exasperating. If you want to stay ahead and not get left behind, you will have to keep your wits about you and not be afraid to ask questions. Enjoy the ride!

• *Thursday 21 September* •

It's important to separate the important issues from the trivial ones today in order not to fritter your energies away unnecessarily. Although you'd like to be able to deal with everything as it comes up, you simply don't have the time. Instead, the only way forward is to arrange your tasks in order of priority. And you will be left in no doubt about what comes top of the list.

• *Friday 22 September* •

Friends will be very important to you over the coming month. You will want to spend as much time with them as possible, and you might also get the chance to add to your social circle, perhaps by joining a new club or organization. Even though you will be kept busy, you need to think about your hopes and wishes for the future and whether these still reflect your ultimate goals in life.

• *Saturday 23 September* •

You are able to appreciate the quality of your life today and you want to savour as many different aspects of it as possible. You have a deeply satisfying feeling that all the pieces fit together and nothing seems out of place. This is especially likely when you consider a close friendship or partnership. You have good reason to pat yourself on the back for everything you have achieved so far.

• *Sunday 24 September* •

Today's atmosphere is charged with emotional excitement and something is definitely in the air. The source of all this electricity might be a strong mutual attraction with a certain person that is becoming almost impossible to resist. You could also be swept along in the wake of some intense but private emotions now. Should you keep them to yourself or confide in someone who will understand?

• *Monday 25 September* •

Take care when talking to partners and people in authority over you today because they could be rather tough-going. Someone might seem over-anxious to point out your mistakes or character flaws, even though they may say they are only doing it for your own good. That isn't the way it will feel to you! If possible, keep away from anyone who is a hard taskmaster at the best of times because they are no fun at all at the moment.

• *Tuesday 26 September* •

You long to keep the world at bay today and give yourself time to take stock of recent developments. You need to sort out a few things in your own mind and you don't want to be surrounded by a lot of people demanding your attention. You may have to get away completely if you want some peace and quiet, and time to think.

• *Wednesday 27 September* •

You could discover that somebody isn't as perfect as you thought today and it will bring you back down to earth with a bump. It's not so much that this person has let you down, more that you have been glossing over their imperfections and now the cracks are beginning to show. If this all sounds very familiar because you've been through it before, maybe it's time to change your attitude in some way?

• *Thursday 28 September* •

You are not quite ready to throw yourself back into the swing of things because in many ways you're still reeling from having to face some home truths. Although you may be smarting, with hindsight you'll see this as a very positive experience because it's helping you to understand yourself better. What you learn from this will equip you to handle difficult situations better in the future.

• *Friday 29 September* •

This is an ideal day to get together with good friends and have some fun. You need the company of like-minded people because you need to feel completely at home with them. You're feeling much more confident about your relationships and you have a much clearer idea about what you want from them. If a partnership has been floundering in the doldrums recently, this is when you can give it a brand new start.

• *Saturday 30 September* •

You play a pivotal role for a friend or member of the family today, and you will give them the back-up they need to make some much-needed changes. Without your support they may have lacked the courage and confidence to go ahead, but your encouragement gives them the impetus they need. However, watch out for someone who may have a less than favourable reaction to your involvement.

OCTOBER AT A GLANCE

Love	♥ ♥
Money	£
Career	💻 💻 💻
Health	☼

• *Sunday 1 October* •

Try to be as honest and truthful as possible today, because if anyone suspects that you're holding something back they will be very unforgiving. Take care if you are expected to make an important decision or give a considered opinion because you may not yet have all the facts. Even if it seems as though you are being kept fully informed about something, someone may actually be keeping you in the dark. If so, why?

• *Monday 2 October* •

It's a lovely day for doing something that you enjoy, especially if you do it with a special person. You might also discover that someone you meet through a career or business matter has a very powerful effect on you. They could make your pulse race or you might wonder if it's right to make a play for them. If you already have your sights set on someone that you know through work, you could be delighted with today's romantic developments!

• *Tuesday 3 October* •

You could be locked in a power struggle today that tests your resolve on every front. The last thing you want is a clash with this person but, because they refuse to budge, you don't have much choice. They seem to be stuck in an all-or-nothing mentality, so that even if you were to concede on a few points it still wouldn't wash with them. It seems that the battle lines are drawn and you have no option but to fight your corner.

• *Wednesday 4 October* •

Your self-esteem is higher than it's been in a long time and you feel that you're operating from a position of strength in everything you do. You will be able to make a very positive contribution to something that you passionately believe in, and you're reminded of how gratifying it is when you can make a difference. Everyone, including yourself, will benefit from your current generosity of spirit.

• *Thursday 5 October* •

'No holds barred' is an understatement for the sort of day you have in mind. You've got enough stamina to pass any endurance test and, if you put it to good use, you'll be amazed at how much you can achieve. However, you will become irritable and short-tempered if you fritter your energies away, so avoid the temptation of doing less than your best.

• *Friday 6 October* •

You want to be in the limelight today and, although you're not exactly elbowing your way to the front, you are determined to promote yourself. You'll score more points if you quietly persist in your quest than if you are overtly pushy. Being in competition with others will give you the motivation you need to reach your personal best.

• *Saturday 7 October* •

They say that sticks and stones can break your bones but words will never hurt you. Well, you aren't so sure today. A spiteful comment launched in your direction will hit the mark, leaving you wondering what you are supposed to have done to deserve it. Obviously, someone has an axe to grind but it's got out of control. It may not even be your fault – this person is probably angry with the whole world and you're a convenient target.

• *Sunday 8 October* •

You feel like a free spirit today and you don't want to be constrained by anything or anyone. Whether this works out in practice is another story because a certain person may want to clip your wings and bring you back to earth. Being realistic, you will probably end up having to compromise. Does this need for freedom signify something deep within you trying to get out?

• *Monday 9 October* •

Your intuition is razor sharp today and you're unerringly accurate in summing up what is going on around you. This can be an extremely useful tool and it will help you to understand not only your own emotional state but also the feelings of those close to you. A family member in particular is in need of an understanding and sympathetic ear, and may instinctively turn to you.

• *Tuesday 10 October* •

You can't decide whether to be obvious or subtle in the way you put something across today. The direct approach would probably be your more natural way of going about things but you have a sneaky suspicion that being diplomatic will work better. In any case, it can't do any harm to think about what you want to say and choose your words carefully.

• *Wednesday 11 October* •

You are in a delightfully happy and sociable mood today. You might even feel more than a little romantic whenever you think about you-know-who. If you can spend some time with them today you'll be walking on air, even if all you do is gaze into each other's eyes. It's also a great day for being with friends, especially if you can go out on the town or do something enjoyable together.

• *Thursday 12 October* •

A latent talent that you had no idea you possessed is about to make itself known and you'll be delighted by how much joy it gives you. Whether it's something that you suspected you were good at or you come across it by accident, you're delighted to have discovered it and keen to develop it. Somehow you'll find a way of incorporating it into your life.

• *Friday 13 October* •

Whose needs do you put first over the next two weeks – yours or somebody else's? That's the question you're struggling with and there's no easy answer. You would like nothing better than to do your own thing but for various reasons you feel guilty about not putting yourself out for someone else. There may be a way for you to do both but first there will have to be some give and take.

• *Saturday 14 October* •

The less routine you have today the happier you will feel. Rather than organize things, you'll be much more comfortable when going with the flow. This may drive everyone else batty because you won't want to be pinned down and will prefer to go at your own pace. A certain someone may still try to organize you, so you'll have to be very firm if you want them to get the message.

• *Sunday 15 October* •

You're feeling very strong-minded today about what's really important to you, and it's beginning to dawn on you how superfluous certain aspects of your life are. Once you realize what has reached its sell-by-date, you can begin to off-load what has become a dead weight. A good clear-out will have an extraordinarily liberating effect on you and give you a whole new lease of life.

• *Monday 16 October* •

You are deflected from your intended course of action today by someone you rely on who's dragging their feet. For some reason they're trying to do a U-turn and renege on the agreement you made, and they're being very elusive indeed about their reasons. Needless to say, this won't go down very well with you and you don't intend to let them off the hook if you can help it. Let them know that you mean business.

• *Tuesday 17 October* •

You're flying high today and making the most of what's on offer. You may have closed one door recently but you're now faced with more than one to open. With so many choices to make at once, you may have to decide which area of your life you want to focus on first. You may not be able to tackle them all at once! When you have made up your mind, providence will help you as you take a step into the unknown.

• *Wednesday 18 October* •

If you're feeling tongue-twisted today it's not surprising. You've got a lot to say, and talking nineteen to the dozen means you're bound to get your words mixed up occasionally. Any attempt to get you to slow down is a waste of time and you only wish you could get the words out as fast as you think them. Whatever it is that you want to say, you feel a sense of urgency in getting it across.

• *Thursday 19 October* •

Take care today because it will be easy to feel despondent or fed up. Why? It could be because a certain person is being critical or harsh, or perhaps you are feeling unloved and unappreciated. Even though you have the reputation for being able to shrug things off and bounce back, today's events are making it a struggle to adopt such a resilient attitude. Instead, you may want to lick your wounds in peace and quiet.

• *Friday 20 October* •

Good news! Your popularity is starting to rise and it will remain in the ascendant until mid-November. During this time you could be deluged with invitations or someone might make it very plain that they think you're the best thing since chocolate. It's the perfect excuse to buy yourself some new clothes or to revamp your image in some way. Yes, it's gilding the lily, but it will be great fun all the same.

• *Saturday 21 October* •

Don't panic if you have a momentary lack of confidence today because you will be able to turn it around, so you can see that there is no need to doubt your abilities. You might even discover some hidden strengths or a new-found determination to see things through from start to finish. There could also be a great opportunity to do some travelling or to learn about a fascinating subject.

• *Sunday 22 October* •

It's a wonderful day for enjoying the company of people you know very well. There will be such a strong rapport and understanding between you that you may feel there is no need for words. Listen to your hunches because your instincts are working well, especially if you have a gut reaction about someone close to home. If you want to relax, you'll love watching a film or listening to music.

• *Monday 23 October* •

Even though you pride yourself on your energy and stamina, there will be times over the next four weeks when you need to take things more gently than usual. This is the time of year when you always need to recharge your batteries, not only physically but emotionally and mentally too. Spend some time by yourself or be prepared to think things through in greater depth than usual. You will feel richer as a result.

• *Tuesday 24 October* •

When logic and intuition do battle, there's no telling which one will win. Today's conflict is particularly tricky because there are equally convincing arguments for both points of view. Your heart is definitely telling you to be careful and take things slowly but, on the face of it, there doesn't seem to be any reason to be so cautious. If you can't decide for yourself, maybe you should get a second opinion.

• *Wednesday 25 October* •

If you're not in seventh heaven today then you'll be on cloud nine! A romantic development has you dancing on air and you're finding it hard to contain your excitement. In other words, no one who comes within a million miles of you is in any doubt of how you're feeling. In fact, your mood is so infectious that everyone around you ends up wearing a smile.

• *Thursday 26 October* •

If you thought you knew everything there was to know about love, today's events are telling you to think again. Whether your partnership goes way back or has only just started, you're about to discover a whole new dimension to relationships. Although this may totally disarm you at first and leave you wondering what hit you, when you come to your senses you will feel glad about what has happened.

• *Friday 27 October* •

Thank heavens it's Friday! You're in the mood to have a rip-roaring time today, and nothing less will do. If you don't have anything exciting or sociable planned, try to change that as soon as possible, otherwise you will miss out on some good times. Ideally, you should take a special someone by the hand and go out on the town together. A very happy encounter with a certain person might make you want to do cartwheels for sheer joy!

• *Saturday 28 October* •

Take a good look in the mirror. Are you happy with the reflection that stares back at you or do you fancy a change? Maybe it's time to do something different with your hair or the way you dress. Choose an image that brings out the best in you and, if that means transforming your style, why not be brave and have a try? If you don't know where to start, think about seeking expert advice from someone you trust.

• *Sunday 29 October* •

You're making some big changes and everyone in your life is having to adjust to them. Although most people are flexible enough to do that, there are one or two who feel threatened by all the new developments. That may be because they are frightened you will leave them behind or no longer have any time for them. If you still want them in your life, this is a good day to reassure them of that fact. Once they feel part of things, they'll be much more accepting.

• *Monday 30 October* •

You've got a twinkle in your eye today and you can't help but feel a simmering sense of excitement and anticipation. There's no limit to what your imagination can conjure up today, and you could come up with some great ideas. If you want to share a secret with someone, choose your confidant carefully. You don't want to discover that your private business has become the latest gossip!

• *Tuesday 31 October* •

You can set your mind to any problem and come up with a solution today. You're thinking in very practical terms and are determined not to be fazed by anything that comes along. This way of looking at things will not only help you to get a lot done, it will also mean you can give some practical support to someone who isn't thinking as clearly as you.

NOVEMBER AT A GLANCE

Love	♥ ♥ ♥ ♥ ♥
Money	£ $
Career	💻 💻 💻
Health	☼

• *Wednesday 1 November* •

You may have to keep a pinch of salt handy today because a certain person doesn't seem to be making a lot of sense. Are they genuinely confused or are they deliberately trying to mislead you? You may have to suspend judgement for the time being, but even so you would be wise not to take everyone at face value now. It could be difficult to follow printed instructions today because they could read like Double Dutch!

• *Thursday 2 November* •

Your way of going about things isn't everyone's style, but you certainly have flair and panache. As a result, someone will be dazzled by you today. What attracts them to you is something offbeat and unusual in the way you present yourself, and they're so intrigued they want to know more. You're more likely to become friends than lovers, and it may take time to discover what you really mean to each other.

• *Friday 3 November* •

If others are tearing their hair out it's because they think you're being inconsistent and they wish you wouldn't keep chopping and changing. It's not that you're deliberately altering your mind every five minutes, it's more that you're confused about what to do. You may not want to let on that you're in such a muddle, but if you do it may help other people to understand what you are currently going through.

• *Saturday 4 November* •

An important decision that you've been grappling with becomes more pressing today and, in spite of the fact that you're unsure of what to do for the best, you can't afford to procrastinate any longer. Your shoulders are probably hunched up around your ears with tension, but you'll breathe a huge sigh of relief when you finally take a stance and you can put this difficult decision behind you.

• *Sunday 5 November* •

Try to give yourself a breather at some point today, especially if it's been a busy week. Ideally, you should put your feet up at home and do as little as possible. A loved one may want to talk to you about something serious, in which case you need to give them your undivided attention. You could also hear from someone who has been a stranger recently or who lives far away.

• *Monday 6 November* •

You've got your spark back today, not to mention your fiery Sagittarian enthusiasm! What seemed an impossible uphill struggle before almost feels like a breeze now. At least one of the plans you made is now underway and you can look forward to getting more of them off the ground. You're very clear about where you're going, and if you have to promote yourself today you'll know exactly what to say and how to say it.

• *Tuesday 7 November* •

You would love to follow your fancy today and please yourself, but family commitments come first. Putting duty before pleasure is what you feel you should do on this occasion, especially if there's a special reason for doing so. Someone may require your support or it might cause too many ruffled feathers if you don't put other people's needs before your own.

• *Wednesday 8 November* •

If you have been dragging your feet about reaching an important decision, especially if it's connected with your long-term hopes and wishes, you are finally able to make up your mind today. You may find that all your ideas suddenly fall into place or something happens that shows you the way forward. What a relief! There could also be an improvement in your relationship with a friend at long last.

• *Thursday 9 November* •

Talk about mixed messages! A certain someone is blowing hot and cold today and you can't for the life of you work out what they think they're playing at. They're either coming on strong or playing hard to get, and it's difficult to keep your emotional equilibrium in the midst of such erratic behaviour. You'll find out what's bugging them sooner or later.

• *Friday 10 November* •

You can strike a wonderful balance today between letting things take their course and giving them a gentle nudge in the right direction. It's not that you don't trust that everything will work out OK, but rather that you recognize when your input can make a significant difference. It's almost as though you've got a sixth sense which is helping you choose when to act and when to watch and wait.

• *Saturday 11 November* •

Today's Full Moon is reminding you to turn your attention to your work and health over the coming fortnight. Maybe you already know what you should be doing, such as finally getting round to making that dentist's appointment or having a serious chat with a colleague? Tying up loose ends at work or putting the finishing touches to a project will be very satisfying and will clear the decks for something new.

• *Sunday 12 November* •

You could feel slightly the worse for wear today. This could either be as a result of overindulgence, or maybe it's one of those days when you simply don't feel at your best. It's hard to muster up the energy to do anything very strenuous, and you might even try to wangle a siesta so that you're horizontal for as long as possible! Your body is reminding you that it needs to be looked after and can't run on empty.

• *Monday 13 November* •

Is it too early to start thinking about Christmas? It's certainly a good day to draw up your Christmas lists and think about what you're going to buy everyone. Over the next few weeks you will be more aware than usual of the power of your money, and what it can buy you. You will enjoy choosing the perfect gifts for all your loved ones, and you won't be averse to buying yourself a few treats either!

• *Tuesday 14 November* •

You'll need all your powers of persuasion today to convince someone of the validity of what you're saying. They could raise lots of objections or seem incapable of listening properly. You won't make any progress with them until you are able to discover why they are questioning your integrity. Once you discover the reason for their reluctance, you'll be in a better position to win their trust.

• *Wednesday 15 November* •

Unlike yesterday, it seems as though everyone is on your side today and any joint effort is bound to be successful in such a mutually supportive atmosphere. You're thinking big and you've got the right people behind you who are prepared to back you all the way. You are holding a winning hand and you have the skill required to play to the best of your ability.

• *Thursday 16 November* •

Look before you leap today! Trust that you don't have to rush into anything and that you can afford to take your time. It may be very tempting to act without thinking things through but will that really bring you the results you want? You've got everything to gain and nothing to lose by biding your time. The last thing you want to do now is make rash or hasty decisions that turn out to be more trouble than they are worth.

• *Friday 17 November* •

Any sort of discussion is favoured today and even the most difficult of relationships can make some headway if you are prepared to talk through your differences. You are able to detach yourself from your emotions and see things clearly, and this will be enormously helpful to you and everyone else concerned. Even if you don't come up with a final resolution, you will have established a positive framework on which to build. Pat yourself on the back!

• *Saturday 18 November* •

Although one part of you wants to lie low today and not have to make an effort, another part of you feels the need to present a more up-beat impression because that's what's expected of you. The dilemma is whether to give in to your need to tuck yourself away from other people or whether you have to cater to other people's expectations of you.

• *Sunday 19 November* •

Look after yourself today because it will be easy to feel disheartened or crushed by the way other people are behaving. The trick is to work out whether you are the reason for their current miserable mood or whether you just happen to be the scapegoat for their current feelings. It will also be easy to let a fear get on top of you or to worry about something that may turn out to be a lot of fuss about nothing, even though it doesn't feel like that at the moment.

• *Monday 20 November* •

Someone you've had your eye on for some time could finally make a move today and dispel your uncertainty about how they really feel about you. You can put your attraction to each other to the test and see if this mutual fascination has any real substance to it. Spending a few hours in each other's company will soon let you know whether this is a relationship with a future.

• *Tuesday 21 November* •

You're so busy that you won't know whether you're coming or going. Any meetings that involve important negotiations should go well because you're able to communicate in a very clear and coherent way. Discussions and group activities will all go well and, if you keep your wits about you, you could pull off quite a coup.

• *Wednesday 22 November* •

You need to draw yourself up to your full height today in order to deal with a challenging situation. It's not so much a case of doing battle, more of showing your strength by defining your boundaries. This isn't as daunting as it seems because you are more than an equal match for your opponent. Just remember to keep your nerve and stick to your resolve. You can do it!

• *Thursday 23 November* •

Someone could make you a proposition today that needs some serious thought before you say yes. Although it might seem like a golden opportunity and one that you should grab with both hands, if you scratch beneath the surface you may find there's a catch. Even though you're not necessarily being misled, you should still make sure that you have all the facts before making up your mind. Don't be afraid to ask some searching questions!

• *Friday 24 November* •

Although one part of you feels that you should be sensible and cautious where matters of the heart are concerned, a different side of you is urging you to take the plunge. A certain someone is stirring some very deep feelings in you and it's increasingly hard to keep on the straight and narrow when a walk on the wild side seems far more appealing. Dare you follow where your heart leads?

• *Saturday 25 November* •

Life is about to take a turn for the better! Today's New Moon is heralding the start of a brand new phase in your life, when you can take the initiative and make things happen. The next two weeks are the ideal opportunity to put new plans into action or to alter your life in some way. Any venture that you launch now stands a good chance of flourishing, provided you have prepared the ground properly.

• *Sunday 26 November* •

If you are faced with a tricky situation with a sibling or neighbour today, you'll know exactly what to say to defuse the situation. Even if a few cross words do pass between you, the tactics you use will prevent the disagreement from escalating. You see no point in falling out with this person and, provided they're willing to meet you halfway, you would much rather make amends.

• *Monday 27 November* •

You would much rather that someone is honest about their feelings and doesn't beat about the bush, but you might be taken aback today by the frank approach of a loved one or partner. They have such strong opinions about something that they may feel there's no option but to blurt out their feelings. Your smile may become a little fixed as you try to cope with the implications of what they are telling you.

• *Tuesday 28 November* •

Luck is on your side today and you have the confidence to move mountains. Sitting back and waiting for things to happen won't cut the mustard, so take advantage of this propitious time by doing as much as you can to help everything fall into place. The only problem you might have is if you overestimate the extent to which fortune will smile on you. Try not to take too much for granted.

• *Wednesday 29 November* •

If the wind has gone out of your sails today you might as well accept the fact that you haven't got a lot of oomph right now and conserve what energy you do have. There are all sorts of reasons why you might be feeling this way, but there really is no point in putting on a brave face because everyone will soon see through it. Try to give yourself an easy day.

• *Thursday 30 November* •

Everything seems to be going well today, and with luck things will tick along nicely by themselves. This gives you a breathing space to take things easy and not have to think about anything very important. Having time on your hands is a wonderful antidote to all that rushing around you have been doing recently, and you'll be surprised by how creative it is to have a period of lying fallow.

DECEMBER AT A GLANCE

Love	♥ ♥ ♥ ♥ ♥
Money	£ $ £ $ £
Career	💻 💻 💻 💻 💻
Health	☼ ☼ ☼ ☼ ☼

• *Friday 1 December* •

It's a case of ninety-nine per cent perspiration and one per cent inspiration today for any project you're working on. Although you may get the odd flash of inspired thinking, most of the time you'll have your nose to the grindstone and will just keep working at it. If you're in danger of losing interest and find it hard to sustain the momentum, remind yourself of the goal you've set yourself.

• *Saturday 2 December* •

A friend or colleague could play devil's advocate today and help you to view your current position from every angle. You may have got stuck in seeing something from only your point of view, and the input you get will give you a much more rounded perspective. Once you've been opened to other possibilities, you will feel freer to make a more informed choice about your current options.

• *Sunday 3 December* •

Are you all set to shout your new-found ideas from the roof-tops? You're in crusader mode over the next three weeks, and anyone who's a willing audience is likely to hear about whatever you are feeling excited and passionate about at the time. Your enthusiasm alone will make others sit up and listen, but do remember that at times it will be politic to keep quiet and let others do the talking.

• *Monday 4 December* •

You won't have to make a song and dance about anything today because your presence alone will make quite an impact. Whatever you say carries weight now, and if you disagree with anyone they will probably end up conceding to your wishes. It's almost as though you are exerting a hypnotic effect on others and they feel compelled to go along with you. However, make sure you don't exploit this ability to influence other people.

• *Tuesday 5 December* •

You are able to reap what you've sown today and see exactly how far you've come this year. You can be justifiably pleased with all the goals that you've managed to attain, and you're philosophical about the losses and disappointments along the way. If there's an area that you're still working on and hoping will come to fruition, do what you can today to help it take shape.

• *Wednesday 6 December* •

It's almost as though you know what someone is going to say before they've said it today, and you can see straight through anyone who's trying to disguise the truth. It could be a mixed blessing to be so in tune with everyone around you, because sometimes you may not like the impressions you get from certain people. On the plus side, you will feel especially close to a loved one.

• *Thursday 7 December* •

You are blessed with some brilliant and far-sighted ideas today, and you can't wait to put them into practice. It will be good to discuss them with other people, especially if you can count on getting some good feedback or further inspiration. If you have been plucking up the courage to have a word with someone, this is the perfect day to do it. You are feeling brave without being foolhardy. Good luck!

• *Friday 8 December* •

Your social life starts to swing from today, guaranteeing a very happy run-up to the festive season. If you haven't already done so, you had better dust off your party clothes because you are going to need them in the next few weeks. Alternatively, how about buying something new so you can knock 'em dead at all those social events you've got lined up? If you are currently a solo Sagittarian, someone you see on a regular basis could soon make your heart flutter!

• *Saturday 9 December* •

A good and reliable friend turns up today to give you exactly the support you need. You feel so at home with this person that you don't need to explain yourself because they already know who you are. They might also make some suggestions that are so wonderful you are champing at the bit to put them into action. At best, this person will restore your faith in human nature.

• *Sunday 10 December* •

You long to devote your day to sheer pleasure, eating good food in the company of dear friends and getting into the right mood for the festive season. You might all decide to go out somewhere special rather than have to cook at home. Take care if you're doing some Christmas shopping because it will be awfully easy to get carried away and end up spending more than you intended.

• *Monday 11 December* •

Even though you are busy enjoying yourself at the moment, you will need to spend time mulling over your partnerships during the coming two weeks. If an alliance isn't going the way you would like, or you sense that one relationship has reached the end of the road, now is the time to do something about it. You may have to declare your true feelings, and you may also have to be cruel to be kind.

• *Tuesday 12 December* •

Not only can you do virtually anything you set your mind to today, you can also help to solve a challenging predicament that a friend finds themselves in. You can somehow get to the heart of the matter without going down any blind alleys and getting lost. Having identified the key issues, you will be able to step back and get on with your own brainstorming session.

• *Wednesday 13 December* •

You could easily win a popularity contest today and you wouldn't even have to turn on the charm! You will be in your element at any social function you attend now, but you will have to spread yourself about if everyone is going to have a chance to talk to you. Being well-liked gives you a lovely warm feeling and boosts your confidence to record levels.

• *Thursday 14 December* •

Some people will find it hard to get through to you today because half of you is here and half of you is off in a dream-world. You will probably be able to operate on auto-pilot and attend to the practicalities, but all the time your mind will be conjuring up a new idea or plan for the future. Those who don't know you well might try to pull you back down to earth, but they'll soon realize they're wasting their time.

• *Friday 15 December* •

You will need to travel at the speed of light today if you want to keep pace with everything that's going on. There's so much to do and, with Christmas just around the corner, you haven't got a minute to lose. Organization is the key between now and the big day, and if that isn't your strongest suit you should get as much help as possible so that you're ready on time.

• *Saturday 16 December* •

You are probably doing some last-minute shopping this weekend, or perhaps you have only just started tackling that long list of things to buy? Try to avoid getting in a panic, even if you are wondering how you're going to get everything done in time. It will be easy to press the panic button and to feel that everything is getting on top of you but you need to maintain a sense of balance.

• *Sunday 17 December* •

Even if you have to work today, you're in such a productive frame of mind that you won't care at all. In fact, you'd much rather get all the outstanding jobs out of the way, especially after yesterday's panic. To operate at your best, plan your strategy in advance so you will make the most of the time available. You will be able to push yourself quite hard and still not run out of steam, so get as much done as you can and you'll feel more than satisfied.

• *Monday 18 December* •

Life tastes sweet today and the day promises to be extremely enjoyable. Conditions at work are favourable and everyone seems to be in a good mood, creating a wonderfully cooperative spirit and enhancing the atmosphere. Your home life also feels very harmonious, with everyone being considerate and helpful. Long may it last!

• *Tuesday 19 December* •

You can manage to withstand a reasonable amount of stress without going into overload today. Although you may have more than your fair share of work to do, you've somehow acquired the knack of juggling it and keeping all the balls in the air. Nothing seems particularly daunting – it's more a case of having enough hours in the day to get it all done.

• *Wednesday 20 December* •

Whatever else you have planned for today, try to set aside some time for having fun. It's exactly what you are in the mood for and, after all, 'tis the season to be jolly! You will have a whale of a time if you are going out on the tiles, but you will also enjoy yourself if you stay closer to home or just have a lively chat with a friend. Someone might do you a good turn.

• *Thursday 21 December* •

Although this isn't the best time to mention it because you are probably spending money in all directions, you need to start paying attention to your finances. Over the next few weeks you will benefit from assessing your current monetary standing and deciding whether everything is hunky-dory. If not, it's a great opportunity to seek expert advice or work out how to improve matters.

• *Friday 22 December* •

This is a wonderful day to give your brain an airing. How about seeing a film, going to the theatre or maybe even hearing a talk about something you're really interested in? Anything that is both entertaining and thought-provoking will fit the bill and will also provide an excuse for an outing. Invite someone who shares your interests and with whom you can have both serious talks and lots of fun.

• *Saturday 23 December* •

With Christmas so close you may well have visitors beginning to descend on you. This can be an added strain when there are so many things to do, and tempers may get frayed. You will have to be as diplomatic as possible in order to keep everything running smoothly, but you'll manage it. If you can adopt a relaxed attitude from the start, you'll have a wonderful time.

• *Sunday 24 December* •

There's a sudden and unexpected flurry of social activity today and there's no way you're going to be able to accept every invitation that comes along, even though you'll do your best. If you've got everything fairly well organized, you'll feel free to go out and have a good time, but if you still have lots of gifts to wrap and food to prepare, you may have to forego some of the celebrations.

• *Monday 25 December* •

Happy Christmas! After all your hard work you deserve to enjoy yourself and have a very special day. And that is exactly what you will do, because you have a tremendous appreciation for the finer things in life today. It will fill you with pleasure and happiness to be with some of your favourite people, and even if you don't believe in what Christmas actually means you will still gain emotional satisfaction from the day.

• *Tuesday 26 December* •

The last thing you want to do today is rush around visiting other people. What really appeals is going at your own pace and not having to make any kind of effort. Perhaps you could persuade the rest of the family to go out for a walk and leave you behind, so you can put your feet up for a while? You might also have been given a good book for Christmas that you are longing to start reading!

• *Wednesday 27 December* •

Your energy levels are building up again and you're ready for the next round of social activities. This time, however, you may feel more like a small gathering at home rather than a raucous night out. You would much rather be with close friends and loved ones than strangers or acquaintances, so what better way to see them than at home in an intimate setting.

• *Thursday 28 December* •

With Christmas behind you, you're already starting to think ahead to next year and what you hope to achieve in 2001. You're in an extremely positive state of mind, and some of the restrictions of this year finally seem to be things of the past. Although you haven't got the whole of next year mapped out, you do have a pretty good idea of what is now possible.

• *Friday 29 December* •

You may have to wear a pair of kid gloves when dealing with someone today. It seems that they have their nose out of joint and they are determined to make other people suffer as a consequence. Perhaps they are feeling lonely or left out, or maybe they are one of those unlucky people for whom nothing is ever right. Do what you can to soothe their feelings but try not to let them make you feel utterly miserable.

• *Saturday 30 December* •

While everyone else is involved in making plans for New Year's Eve, you're thinking further ahead than that and are busily formulating a plan to create more opportunities in every area of your life. Not satisfied with simply maintaining the status quo, you want to make improvements and set yourself new targets. Instinctively, you know that things can only get better in 2001.

• *Sunday 31 December* •

Are you all set for tonight's festivities? Now that you've got a game plan for the New Year, you can concentrate on today's activities and have some fun. You may be more in the mood for a romantic evening *à deux* than a big party, although what might happen is that you end up getting swept along with everyone else's wishes. Whatever happens this evening, you are determined to see the New Year in with a bang!